amortality you and I may share, my Lolita. | But I reckon I go

ne

d it

the

Bookvan

rtle

piano and violin rose u

or me to feel less alone

ne with cries of hate.

Bookvan

ruit of his writings, a

se, absurd histories in books of chivalry, which thanks to th

y doubt will soon tumble to the ground. Farewell.' | Don't eve

r a while I went out and left the hospital and walked back t

to them on the way, in that enchanted place on the top of th

the ring of steel against steel as a far doo— langed shut.

cing. He says that he will ne

pite of thes

he small band of true f

eremony, wer

rne away by the waves an

tance. | Th

e devious-cruising Rach

search afte

r, by your window dreamin

alone. | I linger

the heath, and hare-bells, listened to the soft wind breathir

slumbers for the sleepers in that quiet earth. A last note fro

e slow song that drifted away into the night. Soon the road wa

dust. | The horizon is the straight bottom edge of a curtai

l, farewell to Alexandria leaving. | That was all long ago i

frogs begin and the scent off the mesquite comes strongest.

ybe a little time between, nine months, and now you're dead.

d sheets of paper. First one sheet, then another, blew off th

z," said Dorothy gravely. "And here is Toto, too. And oh, Aur

of the Legion of Honour. | "She's never found peace since sh

sat staring with her eyes shut, into his eyes, and felt as i

and she saw him moving farther and farther away, farther an

is the difference between this and that. | We had the castl

ea hey, you listening? Hey? You listening...? | Terminal. | H

called herself as long as she went on living. And she would c

FAMOUS
LAST LINES

DANIEL GROGAN

CIDER MILL
PRESS

BOOK
PUBLISHERS
KENNEBUNKPORT, MAINE

13-Digit ISBN: 978-1-60433-820-1
10-Digit ISBN: 1-60433-820-2

This book can be ordered by mail from the publisher. Please include $5.99 for postage and handling. Please support your local bookseller first!

Books published by Cider Mill Press Book Publishers are available at special discounts for bulk purchases in the United States by corporations, institutions, and other organizations. For more information, please contact the publisher.

Cider Mill Press Book Publishers
"Where good books are ready for press"
PO Box 454
12 Spring Street
Kennebunkport, Maine 04046

Visit us online!
www.cidermillpress.com

Typography: Clarendon, Garamond, Gotham, Latin Modern Mono, Policy Gothic, Scout, Smoothy

Printed in China
1 2 3 4 5 6 7 8 9 0

First Edition

Contents

Introduction

When I was maybe 10 or 11, my family and I visited my grand-parents. Grandpa Bob was in the TV room with my brother and father, and I was in the kitchen with the food, naturally. As I happily munched away, my Grandma Shelly and my mother were chatting about books when my grandmother said something startling:

"You know, I always read the last paragraph of a book before I start it."

Me: "Wait, what? Why?"

Grandma: "It's just what I've always done. I like reading the last lines on their own."

Me: "Doesn't that ruin the book for you?"

Grandma: "Well, the last lines of a book don't usually spoil the plot. And you know something, by the time I've read 30 pages I've usually completely forgotten what the last lines even were."

I've had many conversations with my grandma, but this one stuck with me. And up until quite recently, I thought her stance was absurd. Why not read the last lines when you get to the end? How can they mean anything without any context?

But eventually, I started looking at them on my own, and saw what my grandmother was getting at: these lines have an entirely separate existence from the rest of the story. Since they will be the final thing the reader takes away, they typically receive a significant amount of attention from the author. Because of this extra bit of consideration, I've found that the last lines stay with you long after you've forgotten the book's plot.

While literature has provided a number of commendable conclusions, no one has time to experience them all. With that in mind, I've compiled the very best endings here, from the famous finishes of *The Great Gatsby* and *A Tale of Two Cities* to the relatively uncelebrated finales of *Memories of My Father Watching TV* and *Rat Man of Paris*. Not every book featured is acknowledged as a masterpiece, but each one closes with something that merits celebration.

Clearly, I have changed my tune since the controversial conversation at my grandparents' house. To my grandma I say: my crow is warming up in the oven. To my readers I say: start at the end.

DON QUIXOTE
Miguel de Cervantes

–

1615

*"I shall feel proud and satisfied to have been the first
author to enjoy the full fruit of his writings, as I
desired, because my only desire has been to make men
hate those false, absurd histories in books of chivalry,
which thanks to the exploits of my real Don Quixote
are even now tottering, and without any doubt will
soon tumble to the ground. Farewell."*

Perhaps the most famous picaresque novel in history, the
ending of *Don Quixote* sees Cervantes take dead aim at the
misleading messages provided by the heroic tales popular at
the time. With his idealistic protagonist continually finding
trouble in the world, many have come to see the novel's last
piece as an attempt to criticize society's insistence on thwarting
the idealistic individual. In a world becoming more and more
realistic, Cervantes seems to suggest that the previous histories
of chivalry are not absurd for the exploits they detail, but for
what the hero is able to accomplish when there is nothing
practical holding them back.

MOLL FLANDERS
Daniel Defoe
-
1722

My husband remained there some time after me to settle our affairs, and at first I had intended to go back to him, but at his desire I altered that resolution, and he is come over to England also, where we resolve to spend the remainder of our years in sincere penitence for the wicked lives we have lived.

The "true" account of a life, Daniel Defoe's tale details Moll Flanders's series of adventures and misadventures. Born in an English prison, Moll leads a wild life that constantly threatens to send her back behind bars. After a series of masterful robberies and narrow escapes, she is sentenced to death after being caught trying to steal from a house. But she manages to convince a minister of her remorse and gets transported to the American colonies with her husband, where her run of exceptional fortune continues. She stumbles upon a farm her mother left her; an inheritance that will provide a comfortable annual income. By the end of the novel she is returning to England, able at last to move beyond the desperation that dogged her throughout her life. And, perhaps, even look back upon the "wicked" life she led.

THE HISTORY OF TOM JONES, A FOUNDLING

Henry Fielding

-

1749

And such is their condescension, their indulgence, and their beneficence to those below them, that there is not a neighbor, a tenant, or a servant, who doth not most gratefully bless the day when Mr. Jones was married to his Sophia.

The incredibly long *The History of Tom Jones, a Foundling* (it consists of 346,747 words), is a coming-of-age tale that follows the life of the titular hero after he is abandoned on a wealthy English estate as a baby. Following a series of bad breaks and misunderstandings that befall him, this seemingly schmaltzy ending is actually reasonable considering the string of events at the novel's conclusion: Tom discovers the truth of his noble lineage, acquires a significant inheritance, and marries Sophia, his one true love.

CANDIDE
Voltaire
-
1759

"All that is very well," answered Candide, "but let us cultivate our garden."

Voltaire once wrote, "Man is free at the instant he wants to be." Throughout the majority of *Candide*, it seems that the exact opposite is true. Fate manipulates the characters in ways that make optimism an absurd notion, and in many ways that is the story's goal (it is a satire, after all). But Voltaire does not want his readers to leave feeling dejected and hopeless. Instead, he ends with an uplifting and practical piece of advice: tend to yourself before tending to the world. This philosophy was initially met with resistance, as it suggested that God may not have made a perfect world. But eventually individuals saw that they were not passive participants in an ideal world, but were free to take agency over their lives, to cultivate their own garden.

THE LIFE AND OPINIONS OF TRISTRAM SHANDY, GENTLEMAN

Laurence Sterne

-

1767

L--d! said my mother, what is all this story about?——
A COCK and a BULL, said Yorick——And one of the best of its kind I ever heard.

This fictional "biography" is frequently seen as an early example of modernist literature, with its use of unreliable first-person narration and digression influencing James Joyce and other 20th-century titans. While there is some argument over whether this is the end Laurence Sterne wanted for his nine-volume opus, or the one that his failing health forced him to settle upon, there can be no debate that the irreverent tone of Yorick's response is a perfect encapsulation of the humor and lightness employed throughout the work.

PRIDE AND PREJUDICE
Jane Austen
-
1813

With the Gardiners, they were always on the most intimate terms. Darcy, as well as Elizabeth, really loved them; and they were both ever sensible of the warmest gratitude towards the persons who, by bringing her into Derbyshire, had been the means of uniting them.

Jane Austen's *Pride and Prejudice* is famous for its highly playful and ironic treatment of English society. Following Elizabeth Bennet as she searches for a wealthy husband—a quest thrust upon her by society and her family's financial plight—Austen deftly charts her protagonist's development from hasty, superficial materialist to compassionate, thoughtful woman. While Elizabeth does indeed end up making a good match and marrying rich, she chooses to marry Mr. Darcy for love, a revolutionary concept in the genteel society Austen was so fond of skewering.

EMMA

Jane Austen

-

1815

But, in spite of these deficiencies, the wishes, the hopes, the confidence, the predictions of the small band of true friends who witnessed the ceremony, were fully answered in the perfect happiness of the union.

Of her eponymous heroine, Jane Austen said: "I am going to take a heroine whom no one but myself will much like." Certainly, the beautiful, confident, and intelligent Emma has a few faults: she is spoiled and slightly smug. But anyone who can find grounds for despising her would seem to be compensating for one of their own deficiencies, such as envy. The end of Emma is a particularly cruel twist of the knife for these folks, as the main character finds true love after a number of failed courtships. In the end, Emma triumphs, and the glory of that victory is clear even to the most skeptical of onlookers.

FRANKENSTEIN
Mary Shelley
-
1818

He was soon borne away by the waves and lost in darkness and distance.

During the dreary summer of 1816, an 18-year-old Mary Shelley engaged in a sort of competition with her husband, Percy Bysshe Shelley, and their friend, Lord Byron. The objective was simple: compose a scary story. Mary went above and beyond, writing a novel that managed to capture the scientific and philosophical anxieties of her own era in a way that still resonates. At the end of this now-mythic tale, Frankenstein's monster casts himself into the cold, dark sea after being unable to stomach all the death he has left in his wake. With his demise he undergoes yet another miraculous transformation: from wrathful monster into sympathetic figure.

THE LAST OF THE MOHICANS

James Fenimore Cooper

-

1826

"The pale faces are masters of the earth, and the time of the red men has not yet come again. My day has been too long. In the morning I saw the sons of Unamis happy and strong; and yet, before the night has come, have I lived to see the last warrior of the wise race of the Mohicans."

The ending of James Fenimore Cooper's historical narrative is bittersweet, tending toward the bitter. The evil Magua is dead. But so are two good guys, Uncas and Cora. Following this final battle between the Mohicans and Hurons, Chingachgook is grieving for his friends and his people, the Mohican lineage of which he is the last. As he contemplates this wretched turn of events, a wise sage named Tamenund sums up the sad state of things, lamenting that the era of the "pale faces" has dawned.

THE PRAIRIE
James Fenimore Cooper
-
1827

"May no wanton hand ever disturb his remains!"

The protagonist of James Cooper's *The Prairie*, who is known only as "the trapper," embodies the spirit of the American frontier. His initial motivation is simple: leave New York and find a place where no trees are being chopped down. After traveling all the way to the Pacific Ocean, his sojourn brings him to the Midwest, where he runs into a family struggling across the prairie. He helps the family relocate their wagons and fight off a group of Native Americans, and eventually settles in a village on the banks of the Missouri River, where his hardscrabble life finally finds peace. Though he dies in this hamlet in the heart of the country, his end is freighted with the nobility he conducted himself with during his life, and his friends pray that the well-earned calm remains with him forever, no matter what becomes of the beloved forest ("noble oaks") where he is buried.

LE PÈRE GORIOT
Honoré de Balzac

–

1835

And by way of throwing down the glove to Society, Rastignac went to dine with Mme. de Nucingen.

Widely regarded as the most important novel in Balzac's *La Comédie humaine, Le Père Goriot* is a marvel of literary architecture, intertwining the lives of three residents of a boarding house: the law student Eugène de Rastignac, career criminal Vautrin, and the elderly Goriot. The primary focus of the story is Rastignac's insatiable lust for social advancement. While he balks at having Vautrin kill a man in order to clear Rastignac's way to a woman's family fortune, he continues to seek out a partner who matches his taste for success. He finds her in Goriot's daughter, the woman he is going to have dinner with at the close of the novel. It is unclear if Rastignac ever found what he is looking for, but he did achieve some measure of status: *Rastignac* is now a French expression for a person who will stop at nothing to climb the social ladder.

THE NARRATIVE OF ARTHUR GORDON PYM OF NANTUCKET

Edgar Allan Poe

-

1838

But there arose in our pathway a shrouded human figure, very far larger in its proportion than any dweller among men. And the hue of the skin of the figure was of the perfect whiteness of the snow.

The Narrative of Arthur Gordon Pym of Nantucket, Edgar Allan Poe's only complete novel, ends in a manner which continues to confound and polarize scholars. Following a harrowing sea voyage that includes shipwreck, mutiny, cannibalism, and an encounter with an unwelcoming tribe, Pym, his shipmate Dirk Peters, and a native drift toward the South Pole. After days of no notable events, a "luminous glare" begins to arise from the ocean. The very next day, the large, pale figure arrives, and no more is heard from the men. The appearance of this supernatural figure in a story devoid of fantastical elements to that point is a subject of unceasing debate. And while the typical reading is that the figure represents death, others have suggested that Poe inserted the figure to assert the superiority of whiteness.

A CHRISTMAS CAROL

Charles Dickens

-

1843

And so, as Tiny Tim observed, God bless Us,
Every One!

Hoping to inspire readers to help the less fortunate during the holiday season, Charles Dickens holds nothing back as he attempts to show the power of goodwill in his famous novella: the sickly Tiny Tim survives, the miserly Ebenezer Scrooge is reborn as a warm-hearted savior, and the Cratchit family gets a turkey to celebrate the Christmas holiday in style. In echoing the cheery message of Tiny Tim to close his novel, Dickens seems eager to get us all to maintain a positive outlook no matter how grim things may seem.

WUTHERING HEIGHTS
Emily Brontë

-

1847

I lingered round them, under that benign sky; watched the moths fluttering among the heath, and hare-bells; listened to the soft wind breathing through the grass; and wondered how any one could ever imagine unquiet slumbers for the sleepers in that quiet earth.

Published shortly before her death at the age of 30, *Wuthering Heights* was Emily Brontë's only novel. After a story in which, according to one early review, "the reader is shocked, disgusted, almost sickened by details of cruelty, inhumanity, and the most diabolical hate and vengeance," the benign ending is a welcome respite. And, though she argued that the dead deserve some rest and peace above everything else, Brontë's masterpiece has ensured that her name will always resound in the halls of literature.

VANITY FAIR
William Makepeace Thackeray
-
1848

Come, children, let us shut up the box and the puppets,
for our play is played out.

Intending to examine the tendency toward literary heroism in his time, William Makepiece Thackeray saddled *Vanity Fair* with the subtitle *A Novel Without a Hero* at the time of publication. A tale of the rivalry between the guileless and passive Amelia and the intelligent but grasping Becky, the novel features an astonishing amount of twists and turns. But in the end, Thackeray widens the frame and reminds us that the characters we have become so attached to are mere puppets, proof that, as Sebastian Faulks said, "the highest virtue a character can possess is interest." If this is indeed the case, Thackeray achieved his end, forcing us to ask why we care so much about these fictional beings and whether things work out for them.

MOBY-DICK

Herman Melville

-

1851

It was the devious-cruising Rachel, that in her retracing search after her missing children, only found another orphan.

Loud, expansive, hilarious, educational, and impossible to pin down, Herman Melville's masterwork is the most frequent response to those wondering what the Great American Novel is. The novel's first line, "Call me Ishmael," is one of the most famous lines in all of literature. But the note Melville strikes with his conclusion is equally pitch-perfect, a solemn reminder of what little remains of Captain Ahab's grand designs. Ishmael is the only crewmember of the *Pequod* to survive, and as he awaits rescue while floating atop a coffin, the reader gets a good look at what comes of man's attempt to bring the natural world to heel.

BARTLEBY, THE SCRIVENER
Herman Melville
-
1853

Ah Bartleby! Ah humanity!

Much has been said about Bartleby, the character who would "prefer not to." Like the reader, Bartleby's boss, a Manhattan lawyer who serves as the story's narrator, struggles to make sense of Bartleby's unwillingness to engage in everyday life. This reluctance costs him everything: his employment, his freedom, and, eventually, his life. Discovering that Bartleby worked in the Dead Letter Office in Washington, D.C., where undeliverable mail is processed, the narrator is stunned by the fitting nature of the job for someone so inert, and can only exclaim at the vexing nature of life and those in the world. Bartleby's resistance has long been speculated upon, with Nobel Prize winner Albert Camus claiming that Bartleby possessed "an absurd sensitivity," and that recognizing how ridiculous daily life was, he had no choice but to opt out of it.

MADAME BOVARY
Gustave Flaubert

-

1856

He has just received the cross of the Legion of Honour.

The gloom at the end of *Madame Bovary* is so complete that one can imagine Gustave Flaubert chuckling at his crestfallen readers. Everyone we rooted for has failed or died: Emma Bovary kills herself with rat poison. Emma's husband, Charles, dies, apparently of a broken heart. Their young daughter, Berthe, is sent to live with an aunt and forced to work in a cotton mill. On top of all that, the wicked pharmacist Monsieur Homais is thriving, and awarded the cross of the Legion of Honour for his contributions to the field of medicine. To drive home his point that the world is unfair and indifferent, Flaubert shifts from the past to the present tense at the conclusion, making the reader's despair all the more real.

BARCHESTER TOWERS

Anthony Trollope

–

1857

The Author now leaves him in the hands of his readers; not as a hero, not as a man to be admired and talked of, not as a man who should be toasted at public dinners and spoken of with conventional absurdity as a perfect divine, but as a good man without guile, believing humbly in the religion which he strives to teach, and guided by the precepts which he has striven to learn.

Barchester Towers is the second installment in Anthony Trollope's Chronicles of Barsetshire series, and it is widely considered the best of the six. A satire focused on the hostility within the Church of England, the novel opens with the approaching death of a beloved bishop. His son, Archdeacon Theophilus Grantly, though grieving, recognizes that if his father should die quickly, he will inherit the position, whereas if he takes his time dying the new administration will appoint their own candidate. Eventually, an outside bishop is appointed, creating the strife that fuels the novel.

The conclusion of the novel is Trollope's attempt to underscore the goodness of Mr. Harding, who was offered the position of dean but turned it down, declaring himself unsuitable. While this type of humility will never be celebrated by the world at large, Trollope, having skewered the grasping, sets Mr. Harding aside as a man worthy of special consideration.

A TALE OF TWO CITIES
Charles Dickens
-
1859

"It is a far, far better thing that I do, than I have ever done; it is a far, far better rest that I go to than I have ever known."

It is not the final line of Charles Dickens's *A Tale of Two Cities* that typically comes to mind when one thinks of the work; rather it is the iconic beginning, "It was the best of times, it was the worst of times," that has become embedded in the cultural consciousness. Set against the events that led to the French Revolution, Sydney Carton, the novel's hero, selflessly accepts death in place of another, and consoles himself with the knowledge that while he could not possibly affect the situation gripping France, he could positively influence the situation of the woman he loves, Lucie Manette, who loves Charles Darnay, the man whose place at the guillotine Carton takes. This sacrifice seems to give him a bit of hope, as he is even able to see a "beautiful city and a brilliant people rising from this abyss" that he has fallen into.

THE MILL ON THE FLOSS
George Eliot
-
1860

"In their death they were not divided."

The final line of George Eliot's *The Mill on the Floss* is particularly weighty. Not only is it part of a Bible verse (2 Samuel 1:23), it appears on the tomb containing the main characters, Tom and Maggie Tulliver. Brother and sister whose differing ideologies force them into a roller-coaster relationship, Tom views himself as Maggie's protector, whereas she feels she can handle herself. Eventually, he sends her away and swears it is for good. But in the end, the world ignores this resolution and flings them together. A flood causes Maggie to paddle out to the mill where Tom is working, and they manage to reconcile before meeting their tragic end—together forever, despite their best efforts.

LES MISÉRABLES

Victor Hugo

-

1862

This stone is entirely blank. The only thought in cutting it was of the essentials of the grave, and there was no other care than to make this stone long enough and narrow enough to cover a man. No name can be read there.

Only, many years ago, a hand wrote upon it in pencil these four lines, which have become gradually illegible beneath the rain and the dust, and which are, to-day, probably effaced:

He sleeps. Although his fate was very strange, he lived. He died when he had no longer his angel. The thing came to pass simply, of itself, as the night comes when day is gone.

While it is best known today for the musical adaptation, Victor Hugo's novel continues to cast a considerable shadow. A massive work that contains essays (that do nothing to advance the plot) on more than a quarter of its pages, Hugo saw it as a complete encapsulation of the world that could be accessed by anyone in it. Obviously, his appeal to the everyman is evident in the finale, with the grave returning to its completely anoynmous state and an existential epigraph that many can sympathize with.

NOTES FROM UNDERGROUND
Fyodor Dostoyevsky
-
1864

But to us too it seems that this will be a good place to stop.

Fyodor Dostoyevsky's *Notes from Underground* is framed as an excerpt from the memoirs of an unnamed, exceptionally bitter man residing in St. Petersburg, Russia. The text is highly philosophical, with the man delivering rambling disquisitions on subjects such as suffering, determinism, and egoism in the first portion of the novel. What narrative there is comes in the second section of the novel, where the narrator has dinner with a group of men that he does not like, sleeps with a sex worker, and fumes over a perceived slight from a local police officer. These few forays into the world only cause him to sink deeper into his furious, digressive state. In the end, nothing is resolved, and one has the feeling that the ranting of this man may go on forever.

ALICE'S ADVENTURES IN WONDERLAND

Lewis Carroll

-

1865

Lastly, she pictured to herself how this same little sister of hers would, in the after-time, be herself a grown woman; and how she would keep, through all her riper years, the simple and loving heart of her childhood; and how she would gather about her other little children, and make their eyes bright and eager with many a strange tale, perhaps even with the dream of Wonderland of long ago; and how she would feel with all their simple sorrows, and find a pleasure in all their simple joys, remembering her own child-life, and the happy summer days.

Lewis Carroll's fantastical *Alice's Adventures in Wonderland* has not gone out of print since its publication in 1865. And even that hasn't been enough to quell the public's appetite: the tale has also been adapted into movies, cartoons, plays, and musicals. Esteemed novelist Sir Walter Besant described it as "a book of that extremely rare kind which will belong to all the generations to come until the language becomes obsolete." The story of Alice falling down a rabbit hole into a world of whimsy and terror ends with her waking to the realization that it was all a dream. Interestingly, the closing lines belong to Alice's older sister, who, after hearing Alice recount the wondrous dream, hopes that the glee and imagination belonging to her younger sister are never diminished. Since the book continues to thrive, it's safe to say that they are still going strong.

CRIME AND PUNISHMENT
Fyodor Dostoyevsky
-
1866

But that is the beginning of a new story—the story of the gradual renewal of a man, the story of his gradual regeneration, of his passing from one world into another, of his initiation into a new unknown life. That might be the subject of a new story, but our present story is ended.

The first great novel of Fyodor Dostoyevsky's mature period ends on an unexpectedly hopeful, happy note. After suffering in abject poverty, Rodion Romanovich Raskolnikov obsesses over his plan to kill Alyona Ivanovna for her money. Eventually, his obsession becomes a reality, and he sneaks into the wealthy woman's apartment and brutally kills her, as well as her half sister, with an ax. The crime does not provide the expected solution, as Raskolnikov stumbles around the city, so consumed by guilt that he becomes delirious with fever. Eventually, the angelic Sonya convinces him to confess, which proves to be the beginning of the redemption Dostoyevsky hints at. Though he has been sentenced to eight years in Siberia, Raskolnikov's moral regeneration has begun, making it clear that hope remains for us all.

LITTLE WOMEN
Louisa May Alcott
-
1869

"Oh, my girls, however long you may live, I never can wish you a greater happiness than this!"

A number of great works of the 19th century affirm the independence and strength of women, but few do so as forcefully as Louisa May Alcott's *Little Women*. Celebrated for its depiction of the nontraditional routes a woman can take and still thrive in society, *Little Women* follows the March sisters, Jo, Meg, Beth, and Amy, along with their mother, Marmee, as they work to support themselves in a Massachusetts town as the family patriarch serves in the American Civil War. The last line belongs to Marmee, who, looking out at her husband and thriving daughters on her 60th birthday, can hardly believe her good fortune—a sentiment shared by those who have had the opportunity to get to know her and her magical family.

MIDDLEMARCH
George Eliot
-
1871

But the effect of her being on those around her was incalculably diffusive: for the growing good of the world is partly dependent on unhistoric acts; and that things are not so ill with you and me as they might have been is half owing to the number who lived faithfully a hidden life, and rest in unvisited tombs.

Thanks to *Middlemarch*, George Eliot did not live one of those hidden lives she pleads for at the novel's end. The book looms so large that a personage no less than Emily Dickinson said, "What do I think of *Middlemarch*? What do I think of glory— except that in a few instances this 'mortal has already put on immortality.' George Eliot is one."

By detailing the trouble the intelligent, capable, and enthusiastic Dorothea Brooke has in navigating a male-dominated society, Eliot was far ahead of her time. And while Dorothea ends up renouncing her inheritance, marrying Will Ladislaw, and having far less influence than someone of her abilities should, her happiness at the novel's end, and her husband's move into public reform, prove that it is the "unhistoric" folks that make the world go round: a truth that continues to cause people to reconsider what constitutes significance.

FAR FROM THE MADDING CROWD
Thomas Hardy

-

1874

"But since 'tis as 'tis why, it might have been worse, and I feel my thanks accordingly."

As is typical of 19th-century British novels, Thomas Hardy's *Far from the Madding Crowd* ends with a wedding. Not so typically, however, that wedding is not particularly happy. Bathsheba, the novel's female protagonist, is a woman who has endured many hardships. At the end of the book, she half-heartedly agrees to marry the male protagonist, Gabriel Oak. It is clear that Gabriel's feelings are stronger than Bathsheba's. To put it plainly, she settles. To add even more insult to injury, Bathsheba could have avoided the majority of the tribulations that plagued her life had she accepted Gabriel's proposal the first time he asked her. But the past cannot be changed, and so the story ends with a glum "it is what it is." All that's missing is a shoulder shrug and a "could be worse."

THE BROTHERS KARAMAZOV
Fyodor Dostoyevsky
-
1880

"Hurrah for Karamazov!"

Fyodor Dostoyevsky saved his best for last. As fellow literary giant Kurt Vonnegut said, *The Brothers Karamazov* "can teach you everything about life." Like much of his work, the book features an exploration of massive philosophical themes, as well as an intricate plot that revolves around the eldest brother, Dmitri, and his feud with his father, Fyodor, over money and their love of the same woman, Grushenka. Eventually, Fyodor is found murdered and Dmitri is the prime suspect, even though there are many who had reason to want him dead, including Smerdyakov, who is suspected to be Fyodor's illegitimate son. Following a lengthy trial, Dmitri is found guilty despite maintaining his innocence to the very end. While Dmitri's fate is uncertain, the novel closes with the youngest brother, the angelic Alyosha, being celebrated by the town's youth. Their belief is that his kind soul points a way forward, offering the reader some hope that the tempestuous Karamazov clan may find some peace and redemption through his benevolence.

THE ADVENTURES OF HUCKLEBERRY FINN

Mark Twain

-

1885

But I reckon I got to light out for the Territory ahead of the rest, because Aunt Sally she's going to adopt me and sivilize me, and I can't stand it. I been there before.

As if *The Adventures of Huckleberry Finn* weren't surrounded by enough controversy, the ending has long been a divisive subject among critics and casual readers. Typically, complaints surrounding the novel revolve around its inclusion of what some consider to be racist content that is inappropriate in the context of a classroom. In this case, however, the complaints focus on the story, specifically Huck's sudden, inexplicable change in attitude. In the work's closing pages, Huck seems to become dismissive of Jim, the slave whom he grew to care for so deeply over the course of the book. Some believe that this regression was the result of Twain taking a long break before writing the end of the novel, resulting in a tonal inconsistency.

THE PICTURE OF DORIAN GRAY

Oscar Wilde

-

1890

He was withered, wrinkled, and loathsome of visage. It was not till they had examined the rings that they recognized who it was.

The plot of Oscar Wilde's *The Picture of Dorian Gray* is alluded to in a number of works. In a nutshell, Dorian Gray is a beautiful, vain young man who comes into possession of a portrait of himself which ages as he remains exactly the same. As Dorian becomes more enamored with his own appearance, however, he grows crueler, and the portrait becomes increasingly hideous. Eventually, Dorian becomes wracked with guilt over the way he has acted and decides to destroy the painting by stabbing it with a knife, which causes him to transform into the very thing he wished to destroy; he is aged, bitter, and dead inside and out. It is a stunning ending, but one which Wilde warned the reader of in his preface: "All art is at once surface and symbol. Those who go beneath the surface do so at their peril."

THE TRAGEDY OF PUDD'NHEAD WILSON

Mark Twain

-

1894

As soon as the Governor understood the case, he pardoned Tom at once, and the creditors sold him down the river.

As is the case with a number of Mark Twain's works, *The Tragedy of Pudd'nhead Wilson* is a humorous, wildly effective satire that exposes the cruelty and absurdity present in the institution of slavery. Valet de Chambre is 1/32 black and sold into slavery, while Tom Driscoll is white, aristocratic, and free. However, Roxy—Valet's mother and a slave forced to serve Tom's family—switches them just a few months following their births. The boy destined to be a slave grows up in a privileged environment and becomes spoiled and unlikable, whereas the free-born future scion is subjected to the horrifying existence of a slave. Eventually, after Tom Driscoll robs and murders a wealthy uncle, the mix-up is revealed and the two are forced to switch roles, a change which proves unbearable to them both. The former Chambre, having witnessed the inhumane treatment of African Americans, finds himself unable to partake in white society. And the former Driscoll, while pardoned for the robbery and murder, is almost immediately sold down the river to experience the life of those he made miserable during his time as a white man.

JUDE THE OBSCURE
Thomas Hardy
-
1895

"She's never found peace since she left his arms, and never will again till she's as he is now!"

The sentiment at the end of Thomas Hardy's *Jude the Obscure* may seem harsh if you've never read it. After all, the concluding line doesn't allow one to walk away with much hope. But it is in line with the remainder of the novel, which sees Jude Fawley go through as much hardship and grief as entire nations do in a century. The pessimistic send-off belongs to Arabella Donn, who Jude met as a child and eventually married. Their joyless union ended in divorce, opening the door for Jude to marry his true love, Sue Bridehead. That would seem to be a good break, but since Jude and Sue are cousins, society ostracizes them for their relationship. On top of that, the two children issuing from the partnership are murdered—by the child Jude and Arabella had together. That is too much to bear for Sue, who believes her children's deaths were divine retribution for her unnatural relationship. When Jude goes to visit her in a desperate attempt to get her back, the freezing weather he suffers through causes a fatal illness. All in all, the novel piles a shocking amount of tragedy on its characters, and Arabella's kiss-off, which is intended for Sue, is consonant with the world's approach to Jude and all he touched.

THE RED BADGE OF COURAGE
Stephen Crane
-
1895

Over the river a golden ray of sun came through the hosts of leaden rain clouds.

Stephen Crane's *The Red Badge of Courage* opens with 18-year-old Henry Fleming awaiting battle against the American Confederate army. During the attack, however, Fleming becomes frightened and flees into the nearby forest, where he is attacked by a disoriented group of soldiers. Injured, ashamed, and without supplies, Henry returns to the regiment he deserted to find that no one is aware of his infraction. Henry turns things around and goes into battle with no reservations, proving himself a capable, brave soldier. Having rid himself of "the red sickness of battle," he stands proudly on the battlefield, ready and willing to face whatever dangers may come and knowing that he has reconciled his past cowardice. In the end, though it is raining and the soldiers make "a bedraggled train," Fleming remains above it, having transcended the terror that dragged him so low. The horrible war wages on, but Henry has finally found his place in it.

DRACULA

Bram Stoker

-

1897

"Later on he will understand how some men so loved her, that they did dare much for her sake."

You can thank *Dracula* for every terrible vampire movie you've ever had to sit through. Bram Stoker's novel marked the first appearance of the now-iconic Count Dracula and provided the basis for many of the vampiric tropes that have entered the cultural consciousness. Obviously, the horrifying aspects of Stoker's work stood out, but the book is also a deeply moving story of the love between the protagonist, Jonathan Harker, and his fiancée, Mina Murray. They battle Count Dracula together, a struggle during which Dracula attacks Mina and curses her with vampirism. But Harker eventually slays Dracula and frees his love from her curse, and they go on to live happily ever after.

MCTEAGUE
Frank Norris
-
1899

McTeague remained stupidly looking around him, now at the distant horizon, now at the ground, now at the half-dead canary chittering feebly in its little gilt prison.

Tabbed by Stephen King as one of his favorite books, Frank Norris's *McTeague* is a grim portrayal of excessive greed and its consequences. McTeague, who was born to a poor mining family, has worked his way out of the mines and become a San Francisco dentist. He marries Trina Sieppe, who wins $5,000 dollars in the lottery (more than $120,000 by today's standards) shortly after they meet. As the two become increasingly more obsessed with the money, they resemble themselves less and less. Eventually, McTeague beats Trina to death and absconds to the desert with the remaining money, where he is pursued by Trina's cousin Marcus. In the end, McTeague kills Marcus but finds himself handcuffed to the corpse in Death Valley, unable to make any meaningful progress. From this spot his money can do nothing and his wits begin to leave him. The canary is a hallucination, a sign that he is in a similar predicament to the caged bird he knew in a happier time, during his life as a miner.

THE AWAKENING
Kate Chopin
-
1899

There was the hum of bees, and the musky odor of pinks filled the air.

A pioneering work of feminist literature, Kate Chopin's *The Awakening* also aided the development of American modernism. Readers have long debated whether or not Edna, the novel's protagonist, dies at the end. But to view it this way misses the transformation she has undergone. Having come to the realization that she could never live happily within the confines of society, she strikes out on her own and shows that her burdens are behind her as she sheds her clothes and swims out into the sea. With each stroke she seems further liberated, until she has to consider nothing other than the pleasant sensations surrounding her.

HEART OF DARKNESS
Joseph Conrad
-
1899

The offing was barred by a black bank of clouds, and the tranquil waterway leading to the uttermost ends of the earth flowed sombre under an overcast sky— seemed to lead into the heart of an immense darkness.

Joseph Conrad's novella would famously go on to inspire Francis Ford Coppola's *Apocolypse Now*, but the author sets his work in Africa instead of Vietnam. The book follows the ivory trader Charles Marlow as he journeys up the Congo River to find a mysterious ivory dealer named Mr. Kurtz, who has managed to transform himself from mere merchant into a demigod. As the boat presses on into the jungle, Marlow becomes obsessed with the problem of doing good in a world where only evil seems to exist. At the end, even though he has escaped the jungle and returned to the civilized world, the darkness has not left him, and he recognizes that all paths are sullied by the grim shadow he encountered on his journey.

SISTER CARRIE
Theodore Dreiser
-
1900

In your rocking-chair, by your window dreaming, shall you long, alone. In your rocking-chair, by your window, shall you dream such happiness as you may never feel.

Country mouse moves to the big city in search of stardom; it is a tired trope by now, but it wasn't anything until Theodore Dreiser's *Sister Carrie* came along. Following the journey of young Caroline Meeber as she moves from rural Wisconsin to Chicago and New York City, the originator of the archetype manages to avoid the sentimentality and cliché that plague so many other novels of its type. The novel was so revolutionary that the *London Express* was able to confidently predict its influential future, saying that the story is "one that will remain impressed in the memory of the reader for many a long day." Though Carrie does eventually achieve her long-held dreams of fame and fortune, happiness remains in that fantasy world that she lived in for so long.

THE WONDERFUL WIZARD OF OZ

L. Frank Baum

-

1900

"From the Land of Oz," said Dorothy gravely. "And here is Toto, too. And oh, Aunt Em! I'm so glad to be at home again!"

Dubbed "America's greatest and best-loved homegrown fairytale," by the Library of Congress, L. Frank Baum's iconic novel has had a storied history since its release in 1900. Though the book once came under fire for promoting female equality and encouraging godlessness, the tale of Dorothy and her magical friends is now widely accepted as a childhood staple, and in more mediums than one. After a magical adventure that saw her encounter so much good and overcome so much evil, Dorothy is thrilled to be back at the simple farm with her family, realizing that the grass is always greener elsewhere. And, even when that grass is a brilliant shade of emerald, there is "no place like home."

LORD JIM
Joseph Conrad
-
1900

"Stein has aged greatly of late. He feels it himself, and says often that he is 'preparing to leave all this; preparing to leave ...' while he waves his hand sadly at his butterflies."

It has been said by many that Joseph Conrad's *Lord Jim* should have wrapped up long before it did; however, when the long-winded story does finally come to a close, it does so powerfully. Jim, who has worked tirelessly to overcome the shame of a previous mistake, gets shot in the chest by his good friend Doramin after confessing that he is responsible for the death of Doramin's son. This tragic end to Jim's tale of redemption leaves the optimistic Stein weary of the world, and provides one with the sense that he will soon follow his friend into the afterlife.

THE HOUND OF THE BASKERVILLES

Arthur Conan Doyle

-

1902

"Might I trouble you then to be ready in half an hour, and we can stop at Marcini's for a little dinner on the way?"

Sir Arthur Conan Doyle's Sherlock Holmes stories are loved by millions, and *The Hound of the Baskervilles* may be the most treasured of all. It is so well liked that it seems remarkable to reflect on how close the book came to never existing. *The Final Problem*, which was the Holmes story preceding *The Hound of the Baskervilles*, was Doyle's intended end of the series, as he had grown tired of his witty protagonist. But public outcry forced him to change course, and he brought Holmes and Watson back to search for a killer, or perhaps a giant phantasm hound. After a mind-boggling series of twists and turns, Holmes and Watson deduce that this fabled beast is in fact a typical dog dressed up with phosphorous. Mystery solved, they are dashing off to the opera as the curtain closes, their famous charm completely intact.

THE WINGS OF THE DOVE
Henry James
-
1902

"We shall never be again as we were!"

It is not uncommon for an artist's best received work to be their least favorite. Perhaps it is the constant quest for perfection, perhaps it is their art becoming tainted by commercialization. In the case of Henry James's *The Wings of the Dove*, it seems to have been the former. In a preface to the novel, James details the problems with his book, ending with the statement, "The failure leaves me with a burden of residuary comment of which I yet boldly hope elsewhere to discharge myself."

The failure James is talking about—he wanted to create a compelling story that was also cryptic and ended up with a multilayered, character-driven tale—is what propelled it to success. Rich with impressionistic prose, the novel went on to inspire a century of writers, making the exit line a prophecy for all those aspiring authors who encounter it.

THE CALL OF THE WILD
Jack London
-
1903

When the long winter nights come on and the wolves follow their meat into the lower valleys, he may be seen running at the head of the pack through the pale moonlight or glimmering borealis, leaping gigantic above his fellows, his great throat a-bellow as he sings a song of the younger world, which is the song of the pack.

Buck, the canine at the center of Jack London's wildly popular novel *The Call of the Wild*, is made for the frontier. After being born in the lap of luxury in California, he is stolen, sold, and eventually ends up as a sled dog in the unforgiving Klondike region of Canada. He quickly adapts to the harsh life, vying to become the leader of the pack and thriving despite poor treatment and abuse. When John Thornton comes upon Buck and watches the dog refuse to travel over dangerous ground even though it will mean a beating for him, an unbreakable bond is formed. Thornton nurses Buck back to health and the two form a partnership that continues until Thornton is killed by a group of natives. After avenging his death, Buck takes up with a pack of timber wolves and, in the end, is finally beyond the reach of man's cruel world.

THE HOUSE OF MIRTH
Edith Wharton
-
1905

He knelt by the bed and bent over her, draining their last moment to its lees; and in the silence there passed between them the word which made all clear.

The enigmatic "word" in the final sentence is referred to many times in *The House of Mirth*. It is the thing which, if captured, could bring Lily Bart and Lawrence Selden together, despite Lily's high-society status and Selden's lack thereof. By the end of the novel, Selden has found the word, but, tragically, it is too late, as Lily has died of an overdose. So, what is the word? Readers have scanned the pages of Wharton's classic since it was first published to find the answer, and various scholars have suggested *love* and *faith*, since these are both things that could have brought the characters together if they were willing to follow them. That means the "word" is less a password than it is a mind-set. It's a workable answer, but like any great literary mystery, it is not the only one.

ANNE OF GREEN GABLES
Lucy Maud Montgomery
-
1908

> *"God's in his heaven, all's right with the world,"*
> *whispered Anne softly.*

Anne of Green Gables has been a fount of hope ever since it first appeared. An orphan, Anne seems destined to a life of misery when even her good break proves to be a problem: she is sent to live with Marilla and Matthew Cuthbert, who originally wanted a boy to help on their farm. But the charming Anne eventually wins the affection of the married couple, as well as many of those she comes in contact with. By the end of the story, Anne has exercised an immense act of kindness by giving up her college scholarship to remain with Marilla, who is paralyzed with grief after the death of her husband. A testament to the power of optimism and perseverance, Anne is able to look out at the world and feel that she is in exactly the right place, a sentiment that evades so many who are so much more fortunate.

THE TALE OF SAMUEL WHISKERS OR THE ROLY-POLY PUDDING

Beatrix Potter

-

1908

But Tom Kitten has always been afraid of a rat; he never durst face anything that is bigger than—
A Mouse.

In a fantastic subversion of expectation, Beatrix Potter's *The Tale of Samuel Whiskers or The Roly-Poly Pudding* sets the rats against the cats. Tom Kitten is a little cat who disobeys his mother and allows his curious nature to guide him into the attic one day. There, he encounters Mr. Samuel Whiskers and Anna Maria, two rats who are hungry for kitten flesh. They are covering him with butter and dough when Moppet and Mittens, Tom's ferocious sisters, come to his rescue. Although he makes it out alive, poor Tom is so scarred by the events that he never has the stomach to pursue his, and all cats' true calling: hunting rats. Instead, he has to settle for bullying mice.

A ROOM WITH A VIEW
E. M. Forster

-

1908

The song died away; they heard the river, bearing down the snows of winter into the Mediterranean.

E. M. Forster's *A Room with a View* is both an exploration and critique of early 20th-century English society, which held class distinction and gender roles above all else. Lucy Honeychurch, the novel's protagonist, places little stock in the expectations of society, but is somewhat kept in line by her domineering cousin Charlotte Bartlett. When Lucy begins to develop feelings for a young man of a lower class named George Emerson, Charlotte forcefully objects to the match. After struggling with what to do, Lucy and George run away to Florence, where they rejoice in their new love and look out upon a river that is carrying away all of the restraint and frigidness from the society they have left behind.

ETHAN FROME
Edith Wharton
-
1911

*"And I say, if she'd ha' died, Ethan might ha' lived;
and the way they are now, I don't see's there's much
difference between the Fromes up at the farm and the
Fromes down in the graveyard; 'cept that down there
they're all quiet, and the women have got to hold
their tongues."*

Famed literary critic Lionel Trilling described the ending of
Edith Wharton's *Ethan Frome* as so "terrible to contemplate,"
that "the mind can do nothing with it, can only endure it."
Indeed, it is a horrifying conclusion to a story of two adulterers.
Ethan Frome is married to the sickly Zeena and in love with
her cousin Mattie. Ethan and Mattie regularly sneak around
together and dream of spending the rest of their lives together,
a world they would be able to inhabit if only the chronically
ill, grumpy Zeena weren't in the picture. Eventually, Ethan and
Mattie see only one solution: to kill themselves by sledding into
a large tree. They go through with it, but the collision cripples
them. With cruel irony, their wish comes true: they end up
living together, but, under the care of Zeena, it is an existence
even less appealing than death.

THE AUTOBIOGRAPHY OF AN EX-COLORED MAN

James Weldon Johnson

-

1912

My love for my children makes me glad that I am what I am and keeps me from desiring to be otherwise; and yet, when I sometimes open a little box in which I still keep my fast yellowing manuscripts, the only tangible remnants of a vanished dream, a dead ambition, a sacrificed talent, I cannot repress the thought that, after all, I have chosen the lesser part, that I have sold my birthright for a mess of pottage.

The narrator of *The Autobiography of an Ex-Colored Man* initially believes that he is white. Once an exercise at school reveals that he is black, he embraces his newfound heritage for a time and uses his immense natural talent to make ragtime music. However, after witnessing the brutal murder of a black man by a crowd of white people, he becomes too frightened to continue living as a black man and decides to live life as a white man, giving up his career in music so that he can use his light-colored skin to fool everyone he meets. By the end, while content to have salvaged himself and his children from the fires of racial prejudice, he is clearly dejected to have sold his abilities and identity for so little—a sentiment that transcends racial lines.

SWANN'S WAY
Marcel Proust
-
1913

They were only a thin slice, held between the contiguous impressions that composed our life at that time; the memory of a particular image is but regret for a particular moment; and houses, roads, avenues are as fugitive, alas, as the years.

To call the final lines of *Swann's Way* an ending would be a mischaracterization; after all, it is just the first volume of Marcel Proust's mammoth *In Search of Lost Time*. *Swann's Way* is in many ways the most significant of the novel's seven volumes, introducing readers to what has been tabbed "the Proustian moment," an intense sensory experience that projects one into a vivid recollection of the past. The narrator experiences one of these moments when he bites into a madeleine that has been dipped into a cup of tea. This bite propels him back, commencing a long journey that is at once dazzling and terrifying.

OF HUMAN BONDAGE
W. Somerset Maugham

-

1915

Cabs and omnibuses hurried to and fro, and crowds passed, hastening in every direction, and the sun was shining.

Desperate to live a life of passion, Philip Carey, the protagonist of W. Somerset Maugham's *Of Human Bondage*, moves past the insecurity fostered by his clubfoot. His desperation pushes him to become an artist, and into several torrid and ultimately unsatisfying love affairs. Eventually, he gives up on his dreams and pursues medicine, a steady profession that leaves him hungry to travel the world. At the novel's close, we see that Philip has let go of what he thinks he wants and accepted what he already has. He is finally content to let the speeding world he once longed to be in the thick of rush past.

THE SONG OF THE LARK
Willa Cather
-
1915

So, into all the little settlements of quiet people, tidings of what their boys and girls are doing in the world bring refreshment; bring to the old, memories, and to the young, dreams.

Willa Cather's third novel, *The Song of the Lark*, tells the story of a young girl whose artistic gifts carry her out of the developing West and into great success. Thea Kronborg grows up in the small down of Moonstone, Colorado. When she is not contending with the hardships of frontier life, she takes piano lessons and develops her beautiful singing voice. Members of the community recognize her talent and rally around her to help her pursue her dream of becoming a singer. Because of the love and support of others, Thea eventually makes it to Germany to study music, and then on to New York City, where she performs at the Metropolitan Opera House. The final lines serve as a reminder that no matter how far you go, what you go on to do will always be felt by those who have remained behind.

THE GOOD SOLDIER

Ford Madox Ford

-

1915

I wanted to say, "God bless you," for I also am a sentimentalist. But I thought that perhaps that would not be quite English good form, so I trotted off with the telegram to Leonora. She was quite pleased with it.

Ford Madox Ford's *The Good Soldier* opens with an absolute, as narrator John Dowell claims, "This is the saddest story I have ever heard." When you discover that he himself is part of it, making it impossible for him to hear it, you begin to sense that this may not be the most reliable narrator. The subject of this sad story is two couples: John and his wife, Florence, and their friends, Captain Edward Ashburnham and Leonora. At first, the relationship between the two couples seems pleasant, but upon further description from John, it becomes apparent that the four of them engage in a convoluted series of affairs, both with each other and with outsiders. This information, however, is skewed by the narrator's unreliability: he has reason, after all, to paint a noble portrait of himself. Perhaps the largest point of contention is the conclusion of the story: John looks on as Edward slits his own throat with a penknife. Or, at least, that is what he relays to the reader. It seems likely that John had a more active hand in Edward's death, but, since we have only "heard" the story, we are forced to take his word for both this and Leonora's pleasure at her ex-husband's demise.

A PORTRAIT OF THE ARTIST AS A YOUNG MAN

James Joyce

-

1916

Welcome, O life! I go to encounter for the millionth time the reality of experience and to forge in the smithy of my soul the uncreated conscience of my race. Old father, old artificer, stand me now and ever in good stead.

James Joyce's first novel depicts an artist coming to the point that he can give himself over entirely to his art. The narrative sees Stephen Dedalus, the novel's protagonist and Joyce's alter ego, come to the realization that he cannot fully inhabit his artistic identity without separating himself from his family, his country, his religion, and his past. As his self-imposed exile begins, he appeals to his namesake, Daedalus, the famed artist of Greek mythology. Hoping that this "old artificer" will always support him, Stephen sets out to change his lot in life and the world at large. It is safe to say, considering Joyce's status as a towering literary figure, that the "old father" assented to this demand.

MY ÁNTONIA
Willa Cather
-
1918

Whatever we had missed, we possessed together the precious, the incommunicable past.

By the end of *My Ántonia*, the novel which is largely considered Willa Cather's first masterpiece, we see the narrator, Jim Burden, letting go of an anxiety that has haunted him and being rewarded with a broader perspective. Having gone 20 years without seeing Ántonia, the friend of his youth, he considers a potential reunion with trepidation, fearing that she will have been broken down by a series of tough breaks. Worried that this picture will tarnish his pristine memory of her, he returns to Nebraska and finds that she is living happily amidst a loving family, and even better than the symbol he has reduced her to. The closing line captures the joy of this discovery, and Jim sees that there are some things, and some people, that the world is incapable of knocking down.

WOMEN IN LOVE
D. H. Lawrence
-
1920

"You can't have two kinds of love. Why should you!"

"It seems as if I can't," he said. "Yet I wanted it."

"You can't have it, because it's false, impossible," she said.

"I don't believe that," he answered.

In the foreword to *Women in Love*, D. H. Lawrence wrote, "We are now in a period of crisis. Every man who is acutely alive is acutely wrestling with his own soul." This struggle informs the entire book, which describes the relationships of Gudrun Brangwen and Gerald Crich, and Gudrun's sister, Ursula, and Rupert Birkin. As the relationships between these men and women blossom, so too does a companionship between the two men. When Gerald passes away toward the end of the novel, his passing has a profound impact on Rupert, an impact that Ursula fails to understand. And, although he is certain there was something between them, Rupert cannot quite understand it either. This ineffable quality is the crisis which Lawrence is concerned with, wherein our failure to articulate what is within does not keep us from pursuing it.

THREE SOLDIERS

John Dos Passos

-

1921

On John Andrews's writing table the brisk wind rustled among the broad sheets of paper. First one sheet, then another, blew off the table, until the floor was littered with them.

John Dos Passos's *Three Soldiers* is a novel of the First World War, following Dan Fuselli, Chris Chrisfield, and John Andrews as they fight in the American forces. Andrews, a young composer who struggles to fit into the strict framework of military life, receives the longest look from Dos Passos. His conflict eventually forces him to go AWOL after the war, and he settles down to a free life in Paris. But he is haunted, and finds that he is also unable to build a satisfactory existence in the world he has dreamed of. Eventually he comes clean about his desertion and is hauled off as the pages bearing his art are effortlessly blown away.

ULYSSES

James Joyce
-
1922

*I was a Flower of the mountain yes when I put the
rose in my hair like the Andalusian girls used or
shall I wear a red yes and how he kissed me under
the Moorish wall and I thought well as well him as
another and then I asked him with my eyes to ask
again yes and then he asked me would I yes to say yes
my mountain flower and first I put my arms around
him yes and drew him down to me so he could feel my
breasts all perfume yes and his heart was going like
mad and yes I said yes I will Yes.*

One of the best-known endings in all of literature is delivered
by Molly Bloom, the lively and inconstant wife of Leopold, the
novel's protagonist. Moving at a breakneck pace throughout
the final chapter (which famously features only one period),
the energy coursing through Molly's monologue provides the
reader with some understanding of why Leopold pushes on
with her. While the prose in these final pages is breathtaking,
understanding it—and the work itself—is a tall task. Some
have suggested that it is James Joyce's way of broaching the
subject of a rumored infidelity with his own wife, Nora. As we
are thrown into the dynamic swirl of Molly's consciousness, it

seems Joyce has again convinced himself, as well as the reader, of the depth, and strength, of her love.

CANE

Jean Toomer

-

1923

The sun arises. Gold-glowing child, it steps into the sky and sends a birth-song slanting down gray dust streets and sleepy windows of the southern town.

Now an essential work of African American literature, the complex structure of Jean Toomer's *Cane*—which bounces between prose, poetry, and play-like passages—is the likely reason that it was largely ignored upon its release. But its depictions of black men and women in early 20th-century America eventually proved to be undeniable. And, like the song of the glowing child, gave birth to something that could not be drowned out by the dreary world. This sunrise follows a number of sunsets that are detailed in the book, a subtle hint that Toomer, a large part of the Harlem Renaissance, believed that a new day had risen for African Americans.

A PASSAGE TO INDIA
E. M. Forster

-

1924

But the horses didn't want it—they swerved apart; the earth didn't want it, sending up rocks through which riders must pass single file; the temples, the tank, the jail, the palace, the birds, the carrion, the Guest House, that came into view as they issued from the gap and saw Mau beneath: they didn't want it, they said in their hundred voices, "No, not yet," and the sky said, "No, not there."

E. M. Forster's classic novel *A Passage to India* is steeped in Indian nationalism and the incredible tension between the Indian people and the British who were occupying and ruling their country. The novel pivots around the friendship of Dr. Aziz, an Indian man, and his friend Fielding, a British man. When Aziz is falsely accused of assaulting a British woman and put on trial, he expects that Fielding will be the one person who stands by him. But, unfortunately, Fielding befriends Aziz's accuser and takes her side in the matter. Though the case against Aziz is eventually dismissed when his accuser admits that her claim was false, the friendship between Aziz and Fielding is irrevocably damaged. The end of the novel documents their reunion years later, with Forster masterfully outlining the impossibility of them ever going through the world together. Instead, they will be forced to go through on their own, unable to overcome its imposing structure.

THE TRIAL
Franz Kafka
-
1925

"Like a dog!" he said, it was as if the shame of it must outlive him.

Franz Kafka's *The Trial* was published posthumously, despite his wishes that the manuscript be destroyed; since then it has been heralded as a warning against the dangers of authoritarianism. In the opening sentence, it is revealed that Josef K., the novel's protagonist, was arrested without having committed a crime. During his incarceration, Josef K. is never told why he was arrested and never receives an explanation as to how the legal system operates. As a result, he spends the entire novel attempting to gain his freedom despite the total lack of means at his disposal. Finally, his confusion breaks him, and he accepts his fate. He is executed, and uses his final breath to shed light on the appalling nature of the situation and the oppressive society that forced him into it.

THE GREAT GATSBY
F. Scott Fitzgerald
-
1925

So we beat on, boats against the current, borne back ceaselessly into the past.

The final line of *The Great Gatsby* is one of the best-known, and most analyzed, endings in all of American literature. As narrator Nick Carraway stares out over the dark Long Island Sound and considers everything he has witnessed while traveling in Jay Gatsby's orbit, he cannot help but notice the difficulty of making progress in a world where the tug of the past is both powerful and incessant. Seeing all of the potential present in his friend's re-creation of himself evaporate in an instant, Carraway seems to believe that the world cannot be transformed, only endured.

THE SUN ALSO RISES

Ernest Hemingway

-

1926

"Yes," I said. "Isn't it pretty to think so?"

In the epigraph to *The Sun Also Rises* Ernest Hemingway quoted his close friend, and fellow literary great, Gertrude Stein saying, "You are all a lost generation." This statement, which came to define those who came of age during World War I, was initially a disparagement of the individuals Hemingway ran with in the Paris of the 1920s. Weary following the horrors of the war, they drank heavily and lived with little regard for the future. Hemingway beautifully captured this band in *The Sun Also Rises*, and the closing line—made by Jake Barnes as he dines with his true, impossible love, Lady Brett Ashley—captures the desperate optimism necessary to get through in a seemingly moribund world, while also outlining the dangers of living a life guided by it.

TO THE LIGHTHOUSE
Virginia Woolf

-

1927

Yes, she thought, laying down her brush in extreme fatigue, I have had my vision.

Perhaps more than any of her other works, *To the Lighthouse* demonstrates Virginia Woolf's mastery of the stream-of-consciousness technique. Moving seamlessly between characters' perspectives and providing alternate interpretations of the same events, the novel forces the reader to contemplate the mystery present in the very act of perceiving. In the end, the tapestry of perspectives has been whittled down to one, and Lily, whose artistic bent has long been in conflict with those around her, finally recognizes that her eyes are clear and trustworthy, that those things they offer are worth articulating.

ELMER GANTRY
Sinclair Lewis

-

1927

"Dear Lord, thy work is but begun! We shall yet make these United States a moral nation!"

Elmer Gantry is a satirical novel that details the hypocrisies frequently found within evangelical circles. The title character is a hard-drinking, money-hungry sex fiend who uses his position as a traveling preacher to indulge in his vices. Using his considerable charm, Gantry gains access to a truly horrifying world where innocent people are sacrificed to feed the desires of a greedy and immoral few. Eventually, he settles down as a Methodist minister with a large congregation, but he continues to be warped by hypocrisy, just another powerful man who is far more comfortable pointing a finger than looking in the mirror.

THE HOUSE AT POOH CORNER
A. A. Milne
-
1928

But wherever they go, and whatever happens to them on the way, in that enchanted place on the top of the Forest, a little boy and his Bear will always be playing.

A. A. Milne's *The House at Pooh Corner* is the author's second volume of stories detailing the adventures of Winnie-the-Pooh and the other inhabitants of the Hundred Acre Wood. This moving send-off would later prove costly for Milne's son, Christopher Robin, who served as the inspiration for the character of the same name. His father's touching treatment caused Christopher Robin to be frequently bullied in his life, despite having matured from the child described in the books. The bullying took its toll, and Christopher grew to hate the beloved books and the man who composed them. "[I]t seemed to me, almost, that my father had got to where he was by climbing upon my infant shoulders, that he had filched from me my good name and had left me with nothing but the empty fame of being his son," he later said.

A FAREWELL TO ARMS

Ernest Hemingway

–

1929

It was like saying good-by to a statue. After a while I went out and left the hospital and walked back to the hotel in the rain.

Following the successive deaths of his newborn child and the love of his life, Frederic Henry simply walks out into the rain and returns to his hotel. This stunningly matter-of-fact conclusion is also stunningly effective, for it conveys Henry's considerable shock in a way that something more melodramatic, and seemingly fitting, never could. It is Hemingway's famously economical style at its finest, giving us the sense that his previously vibrant protagonist has little more life left than his partner. By removing all emotion and description from this send-off, Hemingway manages to express Frederic's mind-set with a fullness that most writers can only dream of.

DODSWORTH
Sinclair Lewis
-
1929

He was, indeed, so confidently happy that he completely forgot Fran and he did not again yearn over her, for almost two days.

Dodsworth has been described as Sinclair Lewis's "most sympathetic yet most savage" work. An exploration of the differences between Americans and Europeans, Lewis does not take sides. Instead, he criticizes both equally, and often at the same time. Samuel Dodsworth is a man of considerable wealth. He retires at age 50 and sets out on a European tour with his younger wife, Fran. Fran falls in with a group of socialites whom Lewis uses to lampoon the concept of European aristocracy, while Samuel is the quintessential American abroad. Their responses are so divergent that the marriage cannot stand it, and they each find a new partner who is better suited to them. But making a better match and finding happiness does not eliminate that all-too-American desire for everything, and Samuel still finds himself pining for the woman he was so pleased to be rid of.

AS I LAY DYING
William Faulkner
-
1930

"Meet Mrs. Bundren," he says.

As Anse Bundren travels to Jefferson, Mississippi, with his family and the body of his late wife, Addie, the reader is forced to wonder who is better off: the deceased or the living. The hardships experienced by the impoverished family on the road are constant, and their difficulties are only amplified by Anse's prideful refusal of any assistance. In the end, they do arrive in Jefferson, carry out Addie's wish, and bury her in her hometown. Once that has been taken care of, Anse gets on with things in a hurry, illustrating his bumbling, selfish ways by marrying another woman. Upon introducing this unfortunate soul to his family, one cannot help but be stunned, and feel that Addie is fortunate to be away from such a man.

VILE BODIES
Evelyn Waugh
-
1930

And presently, like a circling typhoon, the sounds of battle began to return.

"Bright Young Things" was used to describe the young, rich, bohemian crowd of 1920s London, a self-congratulatory moniker that was set up for someone like Evelyn Waugh to come along and satirize. The novel's ending has received a great deal of attention due to the unexpected turn from lighthearted fun to absolute hopelessness, as the novel's protagonist, Adam Fenwick-Symes, finds himself unable to be with the love of his life and forced to serve in World War II after years of extravagant living. While the heavy conclusion seems to be the result of an author looking to put people in their place, Waugh suggested that the novel was just tossed off, describing it as "a welter of sex and snobbery written simply in the hope of selling some copies."

BRAVE NEW WORLD

Aldous Huxley

-

1932

*Slowly, very slowly, like two unhurried compass
needles, the feet turned towards the right; north,
north-east, south-east, south, south-south-west;
then paused, and, after a few seconds, turned as
unhurriedly back towards the left. South-south-west,
south, south-east, east ...*

Begun as a parody of H. G. Wells's utopian novels, Aldous
Huxley's *Brave New World* quickly evolved from comedic
exercise into a masterful depiction of a dystopian future–one
ruled by a technocratic empire capable of engineering human
beings. Drugs and technology keep people complacent within
this new "World State," with the exception of the protagonist,
John, who grew up on the "Reservation" that exists outside of
the World State. The illicit son of "the Director of Hatcheries
and Conditioning," John is dropped into paradise by the
chronically displeased Bernard Marx. As "the Savage" struggles
to adjust to the vacuous society, he demands the "right to be
unhappy." When this is denied, he exiles himself to a hilltop.
But his strange behavior attracts a crowd and eventually causes
a breakdown that leads to John hanging himself. The book's

final warning rings true to this day: in a world controlled by technology, the truly alive will struggle to live.

TOBACCO ROAD
Erskine Caldwell
-
1932

It feels to me like it's going to be a good year for cotton. Maybe I could grow me a bale to the acre, like Pa was always talking about doing.

Set against the bleak backdrop of Depression-era Georgia, Erskine Caldwell's *Tobacco Road* focuses on the Lester family, a down-on-their-luck bunch whose depraved inclinations somehow keep them from arousing any sympathy. The lurid story plays out through the absurd involvements of individuals warped by their insatiable hunger. The novel focuses on the activities of Jeeter, the patriarch of the Lester family, and his son, Dude. Between fits of inappropriate behavior, Jeeter strives to establish a crop to sustain his family, to no avail. In true Lester fashion, Dude attempts to marry a 39-year-old woman and runs his grandma over with a car. After Jeeter sets a fire to clear his land and accidentally kills himself and his wife in their sleep, Dude is left in charge of the farm. He turns toward the task with hope, not recognizing that he is doomed to repeat history.

JOURNEY TO THE END OF THE NIGHT

Louis-Ferdinand Céline

-

1932

It was calling to itself every boat on the river, every one, the whole town, and the sky and the country and us, all of it being called away, and the Seine too, everything—let's hear no more of all of this.

Louis-Ferdinand Céline's *Journey to the End of the Night* follows Ferdinand Bardamu from the fields of World War I and the French colonies of Africa to Detroit at the height of its industrial might. His experiences chip away at his optimism and make him increasingly aware of the darkness at the center of the human condition. When he returns to France and his plans for a lighthearted trip to the carnival are thwarted by a friend's death, he can only contemplate the rushing Seine, the sole purpose of which seems to be to aid everyone in their silent, desperate desire to escape the cruel world.

MISS LONELYHEARTS
Nathanael West
-
1933

The gun inside the package exploded and Miss Lonelyhearts fell, dragging the cripple with him. They both rolled part of the way down the stairs.

Nathanael West's *Miss Lonelyhearts* tells the story of a male newspaper columnist who goes by the name Miss Lonelyhearts. His job is to field letters from the miserable people of Depression-era New York City and try to pick them up with some sort of useful advice, a responsibility he typically falls far short of. The content of these letters, and his failure to do anything with them, cause the columnist to sink deeper and deeper into depression. In an attempt to cheer himself up, Miss Lonelyhearts begins an affair with a woman named Mrs. Doyle, whose husband is the "cripple" mentioned in the final sentence. Their struggle over the gun follows Miss Lonelyhearts's religious enlightenment after an illness, and while the ending is ambiguous, it does not appear that he will get to enjoy the peace that this awakening should bring.

THE THIN MAN
Dashiell Hammett

-

1934

"That may be," Nora said, "but it's all pretty unsatisfactory."

The boozy banter of Nick and Nora, the protagonists of Dashiell Hammett's *The Thin Man*, allowed him to create a new kind of crime novel, one that was equally jovial and hard-boiled. Content to drunkenly careen through an early retirement, Nick is called back into action when a particularly confounding murder lands on his doorstep. The case draws Nick and Nora into contact with the grotesque Wynant family, and their playful bickering provides a welcome respite from this group. One thing that was definitely unsatisfactory for the many individuals who loved the novel: Nick and Nora never appeared in another book, despite possessing enough charm to seem made for serialization.

THE POSTMAN ALWAYS RINGS TWICE

James M. Cain

-

1934

Father McConnell says prayers help. If you've got this far, send up one for me, and Cora, and make it that we're together, wherever it is.

Regarded as one of the great crime novels of all time, James Cain's *The Postman Always Rings Twice* tells the story of the drifter Frank Chambers; his lover, Cora Papadakis; and their scheme to kill her husband, Nick "the Greek." After staging a car crash in which Nick dies and they are injured, Frank and Cora draw the suspicion of a local prosecutor, who arrests Cora and begins working to get the lovers to turn on each other. Eventually, it is Cora who flips, though not to the prosecutor. When she is released on a technicality, Frank, though aware of her betrayal, appears to forgive her. Just when they seem destined to ride off happily into the sunset, Cora is killed in a car accident. While Frank's role is unclear, his final address comes from death row. And, considering his duplicitous history, it is impossible to determine whether this final plea is legitimate or just another attempted con.

LOCOS
Felipe Alfau
-
1936

Then I lifted the hook and flung the window open ...
Spring came in.

Felipe Alfau's collection of eight related stories has a number of possible endings depending on the sequence that you read them in. The book, which details the lives of a number of eccentric characters in Spain, is meant to be a scavenger hunt of sorts: the reader pores over the pages looking for clues as to what connects this seemingly unrelated group of men and women. The eclectic cast includes a former giant butterfly charmer turned salesman, a poet turned forensic analyst, a widow who has become a necrophiliac, and a nun who married her brother. These wacky men and women all gather in the "Café of the Crazy" though what exactly brought them there is a mystery to us, and seemingly to Alfau, who inserts himself into his own story at one point. Sitting and searching for inspiration at the novel's end, the uplifting note struck in the final line suggests that Alfau may have found it. But nothing is entirely clear in this piece of proto-metafiction.

NIGHTWOOD

Djuna Barnes

-

1936

He ran this way and that, low down in his throat crying, and she grinning and crying with him; crying in shorter and shorter spaces, moving head to head, until she gave up, lying out, her hands beside her, her face turned and weeping; and the dog too gave up then, and lay down, his eyes bloodshot, his head flat along her knees.

Permanently in the pantheon of lesbian literature, Djuna Barnes's *Nightwood* stood out for more than its daring content at the time of publication. Legendary poet T. S. Eliot, in his introduction for a 1937 edition, said Barnes's work was "so good a novel that only sensibilities trained on poetry can wholly appreciate it." The novel is centered around the tumultuous relationship between Robin Vote, a European woman with a family, and Nora Flood, an American. When the two lovers move to Paris, Robin is unable to control her considerable passion and begins carrying on with other strangers behind Nora's back. Eventually the two reconcile and return to America, where they take a camping trip together. While camping, Nora loses track of Robin. She finds her kneeling before a nondescript altar in an old abandoned church. Nora loses consciousness, and Robin begins a wild interaction with Nora's dog until her substantial energy finally gives out.

GONE WITH THE WIND
Margaret Mitchell
-
1936

Tomorrow, I'll think of some way to get him back.
After all, tomorrow is another day.

The 1939 film adaptation of *Gone with the Wind* is so iconic that some may not realize the story was a book first. But the novel, which earned Margaret Mitchell the Pulitzer Prize, is legendary in its own right, and the ending is no exception. When Rhett Butler utters the now-notorious exit line "My dear, I don't give a damn" (only in the movie does he preface the remark with "Frankly") and leaves Scarlett O'Hara, she retreats to her family home to gather her energies until she can win back his love. Whether or not she will is unclear, because Scarlett has never been one to dwell on the past—as proven by her forward-looking final phrase.

ABSALOM, ABSALOM!

William Faulkner

-

1936

I don't hate it *he thought, panting in the cold air, the iron New England dark;* I don't. I don't! I don't hate it! I don't hate it!

At one point, William Faulkner's *Absalom, Absalom!* held the Guinness World Record for longest sentence found in a literary work. This sentence (which has since been outdone) came in at 1,288 words. Though this sentence is representative of the novel's labyrinthine structure, it says little about what some believe to be Faulkner's best novel. The story details the rise to power and subsequent fall of Thomas Sutpen, who establishes and operates a large plantation known as Sutpen's Hundred in 1830s Mississippi. The story is overheard and then told by Faulkner's best-known protagonist, Quentin Compson, seemingly before he takes his fatal plunge into the Charles (that incident appears in *The Sound and the Fury*, which was published in 1929). Working with this information, one can see the intense inner struggle which eventually overwhelmed him beginning to take shape

OF MICE AND MEN
John Steinbeck
-
1937

Curley and Carlson looked after them. And Carlson said, "Now what the hell ya suppose is eatin' them two guys?"

In a 1938 journal entry, John Steinbeck wrote, "In every bit of honest writing in the world there is a base theme. Try to understand men, if you understand each other you will be kind to each other. Knowing a man well never leads to hate and nearly always leads to love. There are shorter means, many of them. There is writing promoting social change, writing punishing injustice, writing in celebration of heroism, but always that base theme. Try to understand each other." The separation between those who do, and those who do not, is delineated perfectly at the end of *Of Mice and Men*. After George mercifully kills his loving, mentally disabled friend Lennie, the temperamental and narcissistic Curley and the brutal Carlson fail to see what the wise Slim recognizes immediately—that George has been forced to give up something he loves, absorbing all of the pain he was attempting to shield others from.

THEIR EYES WERE WATCHING GOD

Zora Neale Hurston

-

1937

So much of life in its meshes! She called in her soul to come and see.

Their Eyes Were Watching God initially met with unfavorable reviews. But, thanks in large part to Alice Walker's article "In Search of Zora Neal Hurston," which was published by *Ms.* magazine in 1975, the novel's reputation was resurrected. Today, it stands as one of the 20th century's great works of fiction. Though the novel is typically categorized as a formative work of African American literature, the book is actually more concerned with gender than race. The story follows Janie Crawford as she takes an old friend through her life, her three marriages, and the continual flowering of her own identity as she searches for true love. She believes she found the latter with her third husband, Tea Cake, but after he is bitten by a rabid dog while saving Janie from drowning, she is forced to shoot him. It is a brutally sad moment, and yet in the end the reader can see that it has not broken Janie, that she has come to where she can withstand even the most tragic circumstances.

FINNEGANS WAKE

James Joyce

-

1939

A way a lone a last a loved a long the

With an ending that links up with the beginning, James Joyce manages to transform his huge, enigmatic work into an infinite loop. Interpretations of the story have varied greatly since its publication, but at the most basic level, *Finnegans Wake* is about a family in Ireland. In Joyce's brilliant hands it becomes much more, of course. Some have suggested that the novel's unique structure is representative of history's cyclical nature; some have said that the fragmented writing is Joyce's attempt to mimic a dream state; some have even suggested that the hidden meaning of the text can only be discovered by reading it aloud. Whatever his objective, Joyce's gesture toward infinity has ensured that his book will never stop being speculated about.

THE DAY OF THE LOCUST

Nathanael West

-

1939

For some reason this made him laugh and he began to imitate the siren as loud as he could.

The Day of the Locust follows protagonist Tod Hackett as he moves to Hollywood in order to get swept along by the city's exploding movie scene. Finding a collection of empty souls who "had come to California to die," Hackett quickly comes to feel superior to it all and drifts along while daydreaming about his imagined masterpiece, *The Burning of Los Angeles*, a painting which depicts the city being consumed by a holocaust. At the end of the story, a riot breaks out in the streets of LA, and Hackett gleefully sings along with the sirens as he is ferried away in a police car, elated that his fantasy has become reality, failing to see that he too has become as detached and deranged as those he felt himself above.

THE BIG SLEEP

Raymond Chandler

-

1939

On the way downtown I stopped at a bar and had a couple of double Scotches. They didn't do me any good. All they did was make me think of Silver-Wig and I never saw her again.

Detective Philip Marlowe, the protagonist of Raymond Chandler's complex crime novel *The Big Sleep,* is determined to right the world's wrongs. One dreary night, he gets called to the home of millionaire General Sternwood, whose daughter Carmen is being blackmailed by a book dealer. As soon as the detective begins to snoop around, the world unravels and Marlowe is drawn further and further into Carmen's perilous orbit. Eventually, she attempts to shoot Marlowe. But the detective, having seen enough to remain one step ahead of her, has loaded the gun with blanks. Carmen loses her mind at her sudden loss of control and power, and Marlowe can only turn to the bottle in an effort to deal with what he has seen. Unfortunately, on this particular occasion, the wrongs of the world have rendered this tried-and-true solution entirely impotent.

NATIVE SON
Richard Wright

-

1940

He heard the ring of steel against steel as a far door clanged shut.

Richard Wright's *Native Son* portrays the brutal existence of Bigger Thomas. And while it has been seen as a harmful reduction by some—including James Baldwin, who criticized the book for "its insistence that it is [Bigger's] categorization alone which is real and which cannot be transcended"—the novel did draw attention to the desperate lives that African Americans had been forced into. By suggesting that the murder Bigger commits is inevitable due to the system he has been forced to live within, Wright forces the reader to understand that the jail confining Bigger is not all that different from the structure he was forced to live in out in the "free world."

BREAD AND A STONE
Alvah Bessie

-

1941

You been dead all your life since you was born, he thought, except for maybe a little time between, nine months, and now you're dead.

Alvah Bessie's *Bread and a Stone* is the story Ed Sloan, a man victimized by the Depression and a penal system that has no interest in rehabilitation, no belief in redemption. Forced into a life of crime by abject poverty, Sloan decides to turn his life around at the age of 33. But just as he gets things headed in the right direction and marries, the world rises back up and knocks him back down. He loses his job and returns to his life of crime, eventually committing a murder for which he is sentenced to be executed. As Ed looks out from death row, he can see that this sentence has been waiting for him his whole life, shadowing nearly every step he ever took.

THE STRANGER

Albert Camus

-

1942

For everything to be consummated, for me to feel less alone, I had only to wish that there be a large crowd of spectators the day of my execution and that they greet me with cries of hate.

In the afterword of a 1955 edition of *The Stranger*, Albert Camus wrote, "the hero of the book is condemned because he doesn't play the game." Camus's protagonist, the aloof Meursault, cannot play the game because of the inevitability of death. Because he cannot meet the expectations of traditional society, he exists outside of it and comes to see that not only is the universe indifferent toward him and all living things, he also is unmoved by them. A lifelong loner, Meursault is thrilled to have finally found a companion that shares his outlook. Because of this, he at last finds comfort in the world, and is able to even look forward to the day of his execution, when all those who do not understand will cry out their confirmation of this fact.

STUART LITTLE
E. B. White

-

1945

But the sky was bright, and he somehow felt he was headed in the right direction.

E. B. White's beloved children's novel *Stuart Little* tells the story of a boy who is born to human parents but resembles a four-inch-tall mouse. Stuart matures in many of the ways a normal human would, but always resembles a small mouse, making it immensely difficult for him to find his way. The struggle continues until a songbird named Margalo is taken in and nursed back to health by Stuart's family. The two become fast friends, and when Margalo is forced to flee after a neighbor's cat tries to eat her, Stuart ventures into the unknown to find her. Adventure follows adventure as the little mouse travels along in his toy car. Eventually, he meets a human girl the same size as him. An elated Stuart purchases a canoe and works tirelessly in order to take his date out in it, but when the canoe is ruined, Stuart's despondency irritates the girl. It is a sad scene, but Stuart is undeterred, moving on and resuming his search for Margalo, powered by hope.

ANIMAL FARM
George Orwell
-
1945

The creatures outside looked from pig to man, and from man to pig, and from pig to man again; but already it was impossible to say which was which.

You don't need an advanced degree in literature to see that *Animal Farm* is an allegory. But it does take a bit more knowledge to determine what these animals represent. At a base level, the book can be interpreted as general condemnation of oppression and injustice at the hands of government, and this would be an entirely valid reading. But in writing this book, Orwell had a more specific goal in mind, stating, "Of course I intended it primarily as a satire on the Russian Revolution." A staunch opponent of the Soviet Communist Party, he viewed the reign of Joseph Stalin as the ultimate antithesis of freedom. Through this lens, we can conclude that this iconic ending, where the vicious Napoleon allies himself with pigs and local farmers, is meant to represent the Tehran Conference, a 1943 meeting that led to both the United States and the United Kingdom lowering themselves to where they could support Stalin.

LOVING

Henry Green

-

1945

Over in England they were married and lived happily ever after.

Henry Green's novel *Loving* explores the wealthy Tennant family through the perspective of their servants. Once World War II breaks out, the Tennants are called off for more pressing duties, leaving the house's staff to their own devices. Raunce, the new butler, steps up as leader, and keeps the rest of the servants in line. The personal conflicts between workers are set against a backdrop of international conflict, providing a look at how times of war can color even the smallest interactions. At the heart of it all is the relationship that blossoms between Raunce and Edith, a fellow servant. The ending, which sees Raunce and Edith run off to England and live "happily ever after," has long confounded readers. After all, how could such a subtle narrative filled with ambiguity and complex emotion settle for a tidy storybook ending?

ALL THE KING'S MEN
Robert Penn Warren
-
1946

We shall come back, no doubt, to walk down the Row and watch young people on the tennis courts by the clump of mimosas and walk down the beach by the bay, where the diving floats lift gently in the sun, and on out to the pine grove, where the needles thick on the ground will deaden the footfall so that we shall move among the trees as soundlessly as smoke. But that will be a long time from now, and soon now we shall go out of the house and go into the convulsion of the world, out of history into history and the awful responsibility of Time.

If *All the King's Men* feels overly theatrical at times, that's probably because it was originally a play. Robert Penn Warren adapted the Pulitzer Prize–winning novel from a play he had written called *Proud Flesh*. Though the story transitioned from stage to page, the novel retained many of the original touches of dramaturgy, with the political universe of Willie Stark serving as the setting. But the novel is concerned with more than politics. As Warren said, "Politics merely provided the framework story in which the deeper concerns, whatever their final significance, might work themselves out." Indeed, the novel explores such complex themes as nihilism, Calvinism, and morality, providing the audience with plenty to chew on.

UNDER THE VOLCANO

Malcolm Lowry

-

1947

Somebody threw a dead dog after him
down the ravine.

Malcolm Lowry described *Under the Volcano* as "a prophecy, a political warning, a cryptogram, a preposterous movie, and a writing on the wall." Perhaps this sounds overly ambitious, but the drug-and-alcohol-fueled 12-hour journey that Lowry takes us on does feel larger-than-life. Tracing the life of protagonist Geoffrey Firmin on the Mexican Day of the Dead in 1938, the book begins with the return of Firmin's estranged wife and ends with his death. The end, as the rest of the book, is equal parts absurd and tragic, a combination that Lowry hoped would eventually "explode in the mind" of his readers. Considering the book's esteemed place in 20th-century literature—Modern Library deemed it the 11th best novel of the century—it appears that Lowry's wish was granted.

THE PLAGUE

Albert Camus

-

1947

*He knew what those jubilant crowds did not know
but could have learned from books: that the plague
bacillus never dies or disappears for good; that it can
lie dormant for years and years in furniture and
linen-chests; that it bides its time in bedrooms, cellars,
trunks, and bookshelves; and that perhaps the day
would come when, for the bane and the enlightening
of men, it would rouse up its rats again and send
them forth to die in a happy city.*

It wouldn't be an Albert Camus novel if it did not pose a number of heavy philosophical issues. In the case of *The Plague*, Camus ultimately asks the reader to consider the absurdity of the human condition. The "jubilant crowds" are protected from recognizing this grim reality through their willful ignorance. They are focused only on their triumph over the plague, not understanding that they have only been granted a temporary stay, that the plague, and the death it brings, comes for us all.

CRY, THE BELOVED COUNTRY
Alan Paton

-

1948

For it is the dawn that has come, as it has come for a thousand centuries, never failing. But when that dawn will come, of our emancipation, from the fear of bondage and bondage of fear, why, that is a secret.

The history of South Africa is filled with turmoil and suffering. Alan Paton's *Cry, the Beloved Country* was published in 1948, which also marked the first year of apartheid, a system of institutionalized segregation and discrimination that black people in South Africa were subjected to. The book, however, was finished two years before apartheid actually began, making it an ominous prediction of what was to come. The ending of the story, though tragic, is not without hope. Reverend Stephen Kumalo, the novel's protagonist, climbs into the quiet mountains to reflect on his son's execution, which will occur the following day. Though it seems impossible considering the present state of the country, he knows South Africa will see the light again. Kumalo reminds us that though the night may be long, dawn always comes. Sadly, it was a truly long night for the oppressed in South Africa; apartheid did not end until 1994.

THE MAKIOKA SISTERS
Junichiro Tanizaki
-
1948

Yukiko's diarrhoea persisted through the twenty-sixth,
and was a problem on the train to Tokyo.

Junichiro Tanizaki's *The Makioka Sisters* was serialized between
1943 and 1948, during Japan's involvement in and recovery
from World War II. The novel is set in the years just prior to the
war, with the story spanning from 1936 to 1941, less than a year
before the infamous attack on Pearl Harbor. The novel focuses
on the once rich and powerful Makioka sisters, specifically
the third sister, Yukiko, as she searches for her husband. The
Japanese government condemned the wildly popular novel,
saying, "The novel goes on and on detailing the very thing
we are most supposed to be on our guard against during this
period of wartime emergency: the soft, effeminate, and grossly
individualistic lives of women." But the novel lived on, and
lives on, thanks to the care and sympathy with which Tanizaki
granted these "individualistic lives."

CONCLUDING

Henry Green

-

1948

On the whole he was well satisfied with his day.
He fell asleep almost at once in the yellow
woolen nightshirt.

Henry Green's *Concluding* takes place over one summer Wednesday at an all-girls boarding school in England. It is the day of the annual Founder's Day Ball, and the campus is abuzz with excitement and worry as two students have mysteriously gone missing. Mr. Rock, an elderly professor known as "the sage," is the protagonist of the novel. Mr. Rock bumbles about, mishearing and misinterpreting conversations, deriving most of his pleasure from the odd collection of pets he keeps about his home. He effectively keeps the reader in the dark throughout the novel, since Rock himself is unsure of what is actually being said and, at times, what is happening. While one of the girls is eventually found, there are no resolutions, and no conclusions. That is more than okay with Mr. Rock, who seems to want only to doze through the rest of his existence.

THE SHELTERING SKY
Paul Bowles
-
1949

At the edge of the Arab quarter the car, still loaded with people, made a wide U-turn and stopped; it was the end of the line.

What begins as an attempt to save a marriage devolves into a nightmare as Port and Kit Moresby travel to the North African desert in Paul Bowles's *The Sheltering Sky*. The clueless tourists thumb their noses at the Arab culture surrounding them; Kit wants only to retreat to the comforts of a luxury suite, Port mocks the so-called hardships of the land and longs for more substantial adventures. The pompousness of both characters is challenged when they meet with the very hardships that Port mocked. Port is diagnosed with typhoid and eventually dies. Kit, struggling under the weight of her grief, wanders into the desert and is rescued by a wealthy Sudanese man. Or perhaps *rescue* isn't the right word for it, since he imprisons her in his house and drugs her to prevent her escape. While she does get out of that situation, in the end she is still adrift, and wanders off into the streets of Libya.

NINETEEN EIGHTY-FOUR
George Orwell
-
1949

He loved Big Brother.

Few novels have implanted themselves in the cultural consciousness to the degree that George Orwell's dystopian *Nineteen Eighty-Four* has, with "Big Brother"—the enigmatic, tyrannical overseer of Oceania—frequently invoked to describe the increasing surveillance of the contemporary world. The novel's impact was so great that it led to the coining of another term: Orwellian. Used to describe sanctioned deception and blatantly confusing language, the *New York Times* claims that the word is "the most widely used adjective derived from the name of a modern writer... It's more common than 'Kafkaesque,' 'Hemingwayesque' and 'Dickensian' put together. It even noses out the rival political reproach 'Machiavellian,' which had a 500-year head start."

THE MARTIAN CHRONICLES
Ray Bradbury
-
1950

The Martians were there—in the canal—reflected in the water. Timothy and Michael and Robert and Mom and Dad.

The Martians stared back up at them for a long, long silent time from the rippling water.

Perhaps more relevant than ever, Ray Bradbury's collection *The Martian Chronicles* details the colonization of Mars by human beings. Mars, which is already inhabited, initially proves to be quite hostile. Lack of oxygen, angry aliens, and the absence of established civilization are just a few problems that people must contend with on the new planet. Eventually, though, things begin to look up; earthlings and the Martians start getting along, society develops, and Mars becomes quite comfortable. But once war breaks out on Earth, the humans return to find an inhospitable wasteland caused by nuclear Armageddon. In the collection's final story, a lucky family returns to Mars and destroys the rocket that brought them back so they will not be tempted to go back to Earth. Recognizing that the way of life there was entirely misguided, they look down into a canal and recognize that they have always been Martians.

MOLLOY
Samuel Beckett
-
1951

Then I went back into the house and wrote. It is midnight. The rain is beating on the windows. It was not midnight. It was not raining.

Like all of Samuel Beckett's work, *Molloy* resists concise interpretation. The novel is divided into two parts: the first briefly details the life of the reclusive Molloy, who writes down his thoughts and gives them to a mysterious man every Sunday; the second follows Jacques Moran, a private detective who is tasked with tracking down Molloy. Eventually, Moran exhibits more and more traits consistent with Molloy's personality, and the reader can begin to deduce that perhaps these characters are one and the same. At least, we think that's the case. With Beckett, one can never be sure.

THE CATCHER IN THE RYE
J. D. Salinger
-
1951

Don't ever tell anybody anything. If you do, you start missing everybody.

When J. D. Salinger landed on the beaches of Normandy on D-Day, he carried with him six chapters of a work in progress that became *The Catcher in the Rye*. The novel is, famously, the coming-of-age story of Holden Caulfield, whose cynical view of the world and yearning for the joyful innocence of childhood made him the patron saint of moody teenagers everywhere. Though the notoriously reclusive Salinger never publicly commented on the influence of his military experience upon his work, it has been speculated that Holden's transformation mirrors the author's loss of innocence during World War II. Whatever the impetus fueling the novel, Salinger ended up telling Holden's story to a whole lot of folks: more than 65 million copies had been sold as of 2014.

WISE BLOOD

Flannery O'Connor

-

1952

She sat staring with her eyes shut, into his eyes, and felt as if she had finally got to the beginning of something she couldn't begin, and she saw him moving farther and farther away, farther and farther into the darkness until he was the pin point of light.

Initially, the intent of *Wise Blood* flew right over the heads of many readers. Indeed, on the surface it feels like a rejection of Christianity; after all, the protagonist, Hazel Motes, forms a church called the Holy Church of Christ Without Christ in order to spread his anarchic rhetoric. However, as O'Connor points out, the story is ultimately about Motes's redemption, saying: "Not too many people are willing to see this, and perhaps it is hard to see, because Hazel Motes is such an admirable nihilist. His nihilism leads him back to the fact of his redemption, however, which is what he would have liked so much to get away from." Despite fighting against everything he encounters and driving himself insane, Motes ultimately can't overcome the light within him. This is evident to his landlady, Mrs. Flood, who can see it even within his lifeless eyes.

THE OLD MAN AND THE SEA

Ernest Hemingway

-

1952

The old man was dreaming about the lions.

In what many considered to be a return to form, *The Old Man and the Sea* secured the 1954 Nobel Prize in Literature for Ernest Hemingway. The novella tells the story of Santiago, an aging Cuban fisherman who insists on going out to fish despite having gone 84 days without reeling one in. Much of the discussion about the novel centers around what Santiago symbolizes; comparisons have been drawn to Hemingway himself and even Jesus Christ. In the end, however, Santiago seems to represent the admirable resilience of humanity. For even though his efforts ultimately end in failure, he continues to persevere, content to pass along his store of knowledge and look back at the glory days of his youth.

INVISIBLE MAN
Ralph Ellison
-
1952

*Who knows but that, on the lower frequencies,
I speak for you?*

In a 1952 review of the novel, *New York Times* critic Orville Prescott said this of Ralph Ellison's *Invisible Man*: "the most impressive work of fiction by an American Negro which I have ever read." Though he surely meant this as a compliment, Prescott's offensive statement only confirms the problem Ellison was railing against in his iconic book: African Americans' inability to transcend the color of their skin and be seen as viable members of society. Instead, they were cordoned off, as Ellison was into the coterie of African American writers. What Prescott's prejudice kept him from seeing was Ellison tapping into something both specific and universal with his novel. It is an attempt to advocate for all those who have been robbed of their voice, a far from uncommon condition in America.

CHARLOTTE'S WEB
E. B. White

-

1952

It is not often that someone comes along who is a true friend and a good writer. Charlotte was both.

E. B. White's *Charlotte's Web* is unquestionably one of the most beloved children's novels of all time. The story, which has been carrying out the unenviable task of introducing children to the concept of death since its publication, takes the notoriously frightening spider and turns it into the best friend a person, or a pig, could ask for. Fern, a young farmer's daughter, begins the escapades by befriending Wilbur, a young pig whose life has been spared due to his tiny stature. When Wilbur finally grows large enough to be useful, he is sold to a relative's farm, where he is shunned until he meets a spider named Charlotte. Upon learning that Wilbur is scheduled for slaughter, Charlotte begins spinning calls for mercy into her web, an act which the humans interpret as communications from the divine. Wilbur lives to see many more days, but sadly, Charlotte passes shortly after giving birth to many children. The skillfully told story ends on a solemn yet uplifting note, as the pig looks back fondly on his eight-legged friend.

THE ADVENTURES OF AUGIE MARCH

Saul Bellow

-

1953

Columbus too thought he was a flop, probably, when they sent him back in chains. Which didn't prove there was no America.

In the picaresque *The Adventures of Augie March*, Saul Bellow investigates the idea of being an American so effectively that some claim he helped reorient the understanding of it. At the time of publication, the rise of the "Average Joe" was underway. Bellow's Augie March is a relatable everyman; a Chicagoan born with a middling work ethic, who simply allows the dynamism of America to carry him. In this way, Bellow subverted the American Dream, replacing hard work with luck and happenstance. While some people may resist this appraisal of their countrymen, it is hard to blame Bellow for believing in it. After all, he said that the career-making novel "just came to me. All I had to do was be there with buckets to catch it."

CASINO ROYALE
Ian Fleming
-
1953

"Yes, dammit, I said 'was.' The bitch is dead now."

Ian Fleming's debut novel introduced the world to the now-iconic James Bond. In the novel, 007 is tasked with bankrupting Le Chiffre in a high-stakes baccarat game. As the novel progresses, Bond falls under the spell of Vesper Lynd, a beautiful woman who was assigned to serve as his undercover companion. But their idyllic time together is brought to an end by Lynd's shocking suicide. Through a note, he discovers that she was working as a double agent for the very organization that Bond sought to take down and chose to take her own life rather than betray Bond. While the sentiment is admirable, Bond's icy exit line suggests that he has steeled himself against feeling anything ever again.

THE NIGHT OF THE HUNTER
Davis Grubb
-
1953

And so John pulled the gospel quilt snug around his ear and fell into a dreamless winter sleep, curled up beneath the quaint, stiff calico figures of the world's forgotten kings, and the strong, gentle shepherds of that fallen, ancient time who had guarded their small lambs against that night.

The prose in Davis Grubb's *The Night of the Hunter* is as grim as the lead character, Harry Powell. The narrative, which details Powell's release from prison and subsequent greed-fueled crime spree, is as devoid of hope as a dog pound. Driven by the prospect of locating the hidden fortune of a former cellmate, Powell tracks down, marries, and murders his cellmate's former wife before embarking on a hunt for her children, Pearl and John, who have sensed Powell's incredible evil and run off. Posing as a charismatic reverend and sporting knuckle tattoos that read *LOVE* and *HATE*, one would be hard-pressed to find a more frightening figure than Powell. Pearl and John are safe in the end, but Grubb wants us to remain mindful of the ever-present darkness in the world.

THE UNNAMABLE
Samuel Beckett

–

1953

"... you must go on, I can't go on, I'll go on."

Unsurprisingly, Samuel Beckett's *The Unnamable* is an unorthodox piece of fiction. The last piece of what has been called his "Trilogy," *The Unnamable* consists of a monologue delivered by a nameless narrator. Through his language, the protagonist, who exists outside of plot or setting, manages to forge an identity—for a time. Eventually, the speaker realizes that this will force him to go on speaking endlessly, for to stop might mean that he ceases to exist. In all, it's a breathtaking examination of the ways in which humanity is stuck relying on signs and symbols to perform the one task that can make the world bearable: creating meaning.

THE LONG GOODBYE
Raymond Chandler
-
1953

I never saw any of them again—except the cops. No way has yet been invented to say goodbye to them.

When Raymond Chandler wrote *The Long Goodbye*, he had already written five novels featuring the tough, complex Philip Marlowe. However, never before had Chandler placed him under such emotional duress. When Chandler was writing *The Long Goodbye*, his wife, Cissy, was dying of a debilitating lung condition and his depression often affected the quality of his work. When Chandler did manage to produce good material, it was clear that he was projecting his own feelings onto his most famous character. Armed with that knowledge, the closing lines of the book seem to double as an acknowledgment of Chandler's love for his wife, and his understanding that there are those who you can never really say goodbye to.

LORD OF THE FLIES
William Golding
-
1954

He turned away to give them time to pull themselves together; and waited, allowing his eyes to rest on the trim cruiser in the distance.

Lord of the Flies, William Golding's terrifying tale of what humans can become once removed from civil society, has overcome its initial classification as "rubbish" and became a modern classic. Detailing the exploits of a group of schoolboys that are stranded on a tropical island after a plane crash, Golding uses the novel's two leads, Ralph and Jack, to represent the factions that struggle in the world; Ralph bends toward optimism and community, Jack toward power, control, and self-interest. Eventually, the struggle shatters the society they have been trying to create, and they all participate in the brutal slaying of an innocent boy. While they are ultimately rescued, one knows that those eyes, which belong to a British naval officer, will be in the distance for some time, as the boys will forever be struggling with the memory of what they were involved in on that island.

LOLITA
Vladimir Nabokov

-

1955

I am thinking of aurochs and angels, the secret of durable pigments, prophetic sonnets, the refuge of art. And this is the only immortality you and I may share, my Lolita.

In a way, Vladimir Nabokov's controversial *Lolita* begins at the end. In the foreword, the fictional John Ray Jr. explains that Humbert Humbert, the man whose life story we are about to read, died in prison. He also assures the reader that, despite the horrible actions of the pedophilic Humbert, there is a "moral apotheosis" at the end. This claim, however, was refuted by Nabokov, who shed some light on the reference to the poetic "refuge" that concludes his masterpiece. In an afterword for a reprinting of the book, Nabakov wrote, "despite John Ray's assertion, *Lolita* has no moral in tow. For me a work of fiction exists only insofar as it affords me what I shall bluntly call aesthetic bliss, that is a sense of being somehow, somewhere, connected with other states of being where art (curiosity, tenderness, kindness, ecstasy) is the norm. There are not many such books. All the rest is either topical trash or what some call the Literature of Ideas, which very often is topical trash corning in huge blocks of plaster that are carefully transmitted from age to age until somebody comes along with a hammer and takes a good crack at Balzac, at Gorki, at Mann."

THE RECOGNITIONS
William Gaddis
-
1955

He was the only person caught in the collapse, and afterward, most of his work was recovered too, and it is still spoken of, when it is noted, with high regard, though seldom played.

William Gaddis's encyclopedic *The Recognitions* obsesses over questions of art and authenticity in the modern world. The story intertwines the tales of the artist-turned-forger-turned-ascetic Wyatt, the writer Otto, and Stanley, a reluctant musician. Gaddis thought so highly of the work that he told the *Paris Review*, "I almost think that if I'd gotten the Nobel Prize when *The Recognitions* was published I wouldn't have been terribly surprised." But the novel was largely ignored, and while an influential group of writers have singled it out for praise, Gaddis's staggering work has failed to gain traction in the wider reading public, making his snarky stance on Stanley's compositions a delicious bit of irony.

THE TREE OF MAN
Patrick White
-
1955

So that, in the end, there was no end.

Patrick White set out "to discover the extraordinary behind the ordinary, the mystery and the poetry which alone could make bearable the lives of such people, and incidentally, my own life," with his fourth novel. The expedition was an important one for White, who was struggling to acclimate himself to life in a suburb of Sydney, Australia, following a period abroad. His initial impulse was to criticize the averageness and complacency of the people among whom he now lived, but upon reflection he realized that his life was no more extraordinary than theirs. This commonness filled White with dread, so he used his writing to mine for a deeper meaning to existence. In his words, "I felt life was, on the surface, so dreary, ugly, monotonous, there must be a poetry hidden in it to give it a purpose, and so I set out to discover that secret core, and *The Tree of Man* emerged." In the end, White found that the continuity of life is what gives it meaning.

THE QUIET AMERICAN
Graham Greene
-
1955

Everything had gone right with me since he had died, but how I wished there existed someone to whom I could say that I was sorry.

This Graham Greene novel was published 10 years prior to the arrival of U.S. troops in Vietnam, but, based on what it covers, one might think that it was composed in the belly of that intricate involvement. A parable that details the romantic triangle involving a British journalist named Thomas Fowler, an undercover CIA agent named Alden Pyle, and a young Vietnamese woman named Phuong, the novel forces readers to continually consider what the actual intention of foreign intervention is. In the end, the triangle has been reduced to a more conventional two, as Pyle is assassinated (a conspiracy which Fowler aided in). Fowler and Phuong are able to go on together, but it is clear that the guilt over how he conducted himself within the complex framework will haunt him for some time.

THE GINGER MAN
J. P. Donleavy
-
1955

God's mercy

On the wild

Ginger Man

The protagonist of J. P. Donleavy's controversial novel *The Ginger Man* is Sebastian Dangerfield, an appropriately named expatriate who spends his time studying law in Dublin, stepping out on his wife and child, and involving himself in all manner of debauchery while waiting for the death of his wealthy father. Initially, the book was dismissed as "pornographic." But eventually, the book's literary merits, in particular its satirical treatment of ultra-Catholic Ireland, became evident. Choosing to end each chapter with a brief poem, Donleavy saved his best for last, as his plea was answered: his novel has never gone out of print.

BANG THE DRUM SLOWLY
Mark Harris
-
1956

From here on in I rag nobody.

Bang the Drum Slowly tells the story of two baseball players, Henry Wiggen, a star pitcher for the New York Mammoths, and his teammate Bruce Pearson, a catcher who is ridiculed for his lack of intelligence and skill. Wiggen and Pearson develop a friendship, and when the team learns that Pearson is dying of cancer they begin to treat him differently, providing him with the confidence to improve. But his illness progresses and eventually renders him unable to play. The novel is a beautiful plea for empathy, and ends with what the *New York Times* writer George Vecsey described as "one of the loveliest last lines in American literature, a regret from Wiggen for the way the players made fun of a slow-witted and now-dead teammate."

A WALK ON THE WILD SIDE
Nelson Algren

-

1956

That was all long ago in some brief lost spring, in a place that is no more. In that hour that frogs begin and the scent off the mesquite comes strongest.

In a letter to a friend, Nelson Algren once wrote, "A man who won't demean himself for a dollar is a phoney to my way of thinking." This idea informs *A Walk on the Wild Side*. Set against the backdrop of the Depression-era American South, Algren wrote the story of Dove Linkhorn to make a quick buck. The son of a dipsomaniacal preacher, Dove is a man who received his education in the movie house and whose moral code is shaped only by a consideration of convenience. After being forced to flee to New Orleans, Dove returns to Texas and finds things in even worse shape than when he left. As Dove reflects on a life consisting of little more than women and wine, it appears as though the American Dream has officially been consigned to the past.

JUSTINE
Lawrence Durrell
-
1957

And say farewell, farewell to Alexandria leaving.

Lawrence Durrell's *Justine* is the first volume of the Alexandria Quartet, a complex story set in Alexandria, Egypt, during the 1930s and '40s. The narrator is an unnamed impoverished Irish writer who tells the story of the time he spent with Justine, a beautiful Jewish woman he fell in love with during his time there. As the love affair between the narrator and Justine grows more passionate, so too does the danger that surrounds them. By the end, our protagonist fears that Justine's husband, Nessim, may plan to have him killed. He leaves the city, only to return and selflessly allow Nessim to regain his love. The book concludes on a translation of a poem by Constantine Cavafy, the poet laureate of Alexandria. Cavafy uses the poem to capture the regret of love lost, and the narrator hands his translation of it to Justine upon their parting, knowing that without her the city he knew and loved has ceased to exist.

ON THE ROAD

Jack Kerouac

-

1957

*So in America when the sun goes down and I sit on
the old broken-down river pier watching the long,
long skies over New Jersey and sense all that raw
land that rolls in one unbelievable huge bulge over
to the West Coast, and all that road going, all the
people dreaming in the immensity of it, and in Iowa
I know by now the children must be crying in the
land where they let the children cry, and tonight the
stars'll be out, and don't you know that God is Pooh
Bear? the evening star must be drooping and shedding
her sparkler dims on the prairie, which is just before
the coming of complete night that blesses the earth,
darkens all rivers, cups the peaks and folds the final
shore in, and nobody, nobody knows what's going to
happen to anybody besides the forlorn rags of growing
old, I think of Dean Moriarty, I even think of Old
Dean Moriarty the father we never found, I think of
Dean Moriarty.*

Regardless of what you think of Jack Kerouac's countercultural
touchstone *On the Road*, the concluding paragraph is an
achingly beautiful piece of writing. A poem that explodes from

the narrative and manages to capture the energy and approach of the Beat Generation, Kerouac's alter ego Sal Paradise cannot keep himself from thinking of that sprawling country which he crawled over in search of himself and the truth. Though he failed to find to any satisfying answers during those forays, his search—and the verve he and Dean Moriarity approached it with—inspired millions of others to become seekers.

THE TEMPLE OF GOLD
William Goldman
-
1957

I left him there.

Written in three weeks during the summer after he graduated from college, William Goldman's *The Temple of Gold* is a tale of growing up and coming to terms with the events of youth. Raymond Euripides is the central character of the novel. He and his best friend Zock spend their days goofing off and engaging in casual acts of rebellion. Their paths diverge as Zock goes to Harvard and Ray parties. One night, Ray gets into an accident that results in Zock's death. From that point forward, Ray commits to lead a life Zock would have been proud of. He joins the military, is honored as a hero, and upon returning home decides to go to college, something which he was previously too immature to do. Just before leaving, he pays one last visit to Zock's grave, where he has the final conversation that they never got to have. When he leaves, he has finally left the past behind and is ready to live the life he has managed to build.

A NOVEL OF THANK YOU

Gertrude Stein

-

1958

This is the difference between this and that.

Published 12 years after Gertrude Stein's death, *A Novel of Thank You* was written in the 1920s, at the height of "the lost generation" that Stein famously mentored and named. The book is Stein's critique of herself, a deep examination of the writer's role and the process of writing. As such, the book is more of a meditation on the formulation of narrative and how it shapes the world we live in than a traditional novel, and the ending provides no closure. It is only a celebration of distinction, the kind Stein built her existence, and influence, upon.

THE END OF THE ROAD
John Barth
-
1958

Terminal.

Described as "a novel of ideas," John Barth's *The End of the Road* muses on emptiness in contemporary America, and how the abundance of options can lead to psychological paralysis. This notion is embodied by the novel's protagonist, Jacob Horner, who suffers from a condition called cosmoposis, which allows him to view all available paths simultaneously, an omniscience which proves to be a curse. At the novel's end, when his lover perishes due to a botched abortion conducted by a physician Horner has procured, he finds himself once again at a crossroads, unable to move.

CANDY

Terry Southern and Mason Hoffenberg
-
1958

GOOD GRIEF—IT'S DADDY!

Rarely does erotica reach the point where it is considered literature, but *Candy* is one of those exceptions. A novel detailing the sexual escapades of an 18-year-old girl, it was written as a collaboration between Terry Southern and Mason Hoffenberg. The pair received $500 from Olympia Press for the manuscript, which they composed by exchanging letters. The nominal fee left Southern unprepared for the book's impact, as he recalled in the *Paris Review*. "One guy wrote a review about how *Candy* was a satire on *Candide*. So right away I went back and reread Voltaire to see if he was right. That's what happens to you. It's as if you vomit in the gutter and everybody starts saying it's the greatest new art form, so you go back to see it, and, by God, you have to agree." It would appear that the old adage of one man's trash being another man's treasure is true after all.

THE TIN DRUM

Günter Grass

-

1959

Here's the black, wicked Witch.

Ha! ha! ha!

Stuck inside an insane asylum, Oskar Matzerath, the protagonist of Günter Grass's *The Tin Drum*, is clearly not the most reliable narrator. From the jump, he tells us that only by taking us to the very beginning can we truly understand his story. Oskar grew up in Nazi-occupied Poland, a time when death and violence were part of everyday reality. In order to cope with the events of the war and his bothersome family, Oskar would play a tin drum, which he believed granted him powers. He also claims to have stopped growing at age three, upon hearing his father claim that he would grow up to be a grocer. Despite his small stature, he tells us that he led an outsize existence in West Germany: joining a gang, working as a nude model, hypnotizing crowds with his drum, sleeping with numerous women, claiming to be both Jesus and Satan, and eventually getting himself arrested for the murder of a woman, which purportedly landed him in the asylum. By the end, he is left marveling at death's continual presence in his life, feeling it is only a matter of time before the "black, wicked Witch" comes nipping at his heels.

THE BARON IN THE TREES
Italo Calvino

-

1959

That mesh of leaves and twigs of fork and froth, minute and endless, with the sky glimpsed only in sudden specks and splinters, perhaps it was only there so that my brother could pass through it with his tomtit's thread, was embroidered on nothing, like this thread of ink which I have let run on for page after page, swarming with cancellations, corrections, doodles, blots and gaps, bursting at times into clear big berries, coagulating at others into piles of tiny starry seeds, then twisting away, forking off, surrounding buds of phrases with frameworks of leaves and clouds, then interweaving again, and so running on and on and on until it splutters and bursts into a last senseless cluster of words, ideas, dreams, and so ends.

Italo Calvino's *The Baron in the Trees* is the story of Cosimo Piovasco di Rondò, the 12-year-old son of an 18th-century family of Italian nobles. On a rebellious lark, Cosimo decides to climb a tree and spend the rest of his life living amongst the leaves. Once up there, the arboreal world expands into Ombrosa, a breathtaking realm where all of his needs are no more than a few branches away. The newly independent boy quickly embarks on a series of adventures, fighting wolves, courting young women, and even dabbling in diplomatic affairs. He stays there until his old age, when, in his dying days, he makes good on his promise to never touch the ground again, grabs hold of a passing balloon, and sails away to perish elsewhere. His remarkable life is related to us by his younger brother, Biagio, who at the end can only marvel at the unique, impossible existence Cosimo led.

NAKED LUNCH
William S. Burroughs
-
1959

No glot ... C'lom Fliday.

Written as he was in the throes of heroin addiction, William S. Burroughs's novel ultimately has the effect of a bad trip: a long descent into madness and an abrupt stop, abandoning the reader in a swirling chaos. A collection of extremely loosely connected vignettes, the book has been praised for its experimental style and complete disregard for conventional narrative. Like much of what precedes it, the ending of *Naked Lunch* is initially nonsensical, and then unsettling upon a closer look, since it plays upon a cruel stereotype of Asians' accents when speaking in English.

RABBIT, RUN
John Updike
-
1960

Ah: runs. Runs.

John Updike's *Rabbit, Run* is written in the present tense, granting the book the ability to keep up with its protagonist, Harry "Rabbit" Angstrom, a former basketball star who one day decides to leave his young family in search of meaning. Updike commented on his unorthodox choice of tense in an interview with the *Paris Review*, saying: "You can move between minds, between thoughts and objects and events with a curious ease not available to the past tense. I don't know if it is clear to the reader as it is to the person writing, but there are kinds of poetry, kinds of music you can strike off in the present tense." The decision gives the reader the sense that they are simply breezing along with Rabbit, with neither one knowing what will happen. This feeling is only amplified when in the end, as expected, Rabbit runs once more. For this reason, the "Ah," should be taken as a sigh of recognition. Because really, what else is there for Rabbit to do?

TO KILL A MOCKINGBIRD
Harper Lee

-

1960

He turned out the light and went into Jem's room. He would be there all night, and he would be there when Jem waked up in the morning.

Harper Lee only needed one novel to earn a spot at the table of great American writers. That may seem ridiculous, but *To Kill a Mockingbird*, which explores racism in the South, primarily through the eyes of children, is more than enough. Long praised for its handling of sensitive subject matter and the character of Atticus Finch, the book has achieved a sort of mythological status as the embodiment of good. A 1991 study found that *To Kill a Mockingbird* came in second place in the category of books "most often cited as making a difference," behind only the Bible. The book closes with Atticus standing by his son's bed, an image that provides the reader assurance that the virtues he represents will remain forever.

THE MOVIEGOER
Walker Percy
-
1961

I watch her walk toward St. Charles, cape jasmine held against her cheek, until my brothers and sisters call out behind me.

The Moviegoer, the existentialist debut of Walker Percy, follows Binx Bolling, a young New Orleans native who glides through life desperate to stumble upon a purpose. Many critics draw parallels between *The Moviegoer* and the work of Søren Kierkegaard, who believed that the mundane nature of life can only be countered by continually examining and pondering it. Binx's experience in the Korean War has thwarted his capacity for such introspection, and he finds himself struggling to deal with a world that fails to match up to the movies he hungrily consumes. In the end, he decides to create purpose by becoming a doctor and getting engaged to a woman named Kate. He has decided to focus on family rather than his own identity, a decision that foists the ambiguity he has struggled with onto the reader, who cannot be sure that Binx's conventional move will ultimately be a happy one.

CATCH-22
Joseph Heller
–
1961

*The knife came down, missing him by inches,
and he took off.*

Air Force bombardier Captain John Yossarian, the protagonist of *Catch-22*, inquires as to how one might go about getting out of a particularly dangerous mission. He is told that in order to get out of a mission, one must simply admit that they are insane. However, the very act of opting out of a dangerous mission proves sanity, because only an insane person would want to fly in combat; thus, catch-22, which is a military regulation invented by author Joseph Heller. When Heller first wrote his novel, he had dubbed this regulation "catch-18." But before Heller's book was released, Leon Uris's *Mila 18* arrived in bookstores. The last-minute change proved fortuitous, as the catchy cadence used to describe this bit of circular logic helped ingrain the coinage in the cultural consciousness. The end of the novel, which chronologically takes place at the beginning, details the death of Snowden, one of Yossarian's fellow crew members, a traumatic incident which incites the almost-hallucinogenic events that comprise the story.

ONE FLEW OVER THE CUCKOO'S NEST

Ken Kesey

-

1962

I been away a long time.

Though Ken Kesey's *One Flew Over the Cuckoo's Nest* ends in the defeat of renegade psychiatric patient McMurphy through lobotomy, the fate of the novel's narrator, "Chief" Bromden is far more uplifting. Following in the footsteps of the once-rebellious McMurphy, Chief decides to take matters into his own hands. He smothers McMurphy with a pillow, thus setting him free of the hospital's tyranny, and smashes a window with a water fountain, freeing himself. That final page has Chief reflecting on all that he will see outside the prison-like facility's walls; it has, after all, been many years since he was a part of the real world.

A CLOCKWORK ORANGE

Anthony Burgess

-

1962

And so farewell from your little droog. And to all others in this story profound shooms of lip-music brrrrr. And they can kiss my sharries. But you, O my brothers, remember sometimes thy little Alex that was. Amen. And all that cal.

While the controversy surrounding Anthony Burgess's *A Clockwork Orange* typically centers around the book's explicit content, there is a smaller controversy surrounding the quality of its ending. The story, which details the lives of 15-year-old Alex and his gang in dystopian England, ends in a way that is out of sync with the rest of the novel. Alex, after committing heinous crimes, undergoes intense aversion therapy and decides to clean up his act. And that's about it. Regarding his ending, Burgess said, "He grows bored with violence and recognizes that human energy is better expended on creation than destruction. My young hoodlum comes to the revelation of the need to get something done in life." Of course, the ending is not without its merits: it does provide an immense amount of closure. For some, it seems to be more closure than this wild story, and its wicked main character, deserve.

WHERE THE WILD THINGS ARE

Maurice Sendak

-

1963

*Max stepped into his private boat and waved goodbye
and sailed back over a year and in and out of weeks
and through a day and into the night of his very own
room where he found his supper waiting for him—
and it was still hot.*

According to Maurice Sendak, the publishers of *Where the Wild Things Are* took great issue with the final word of the 338-word story. To them, "hot" was too violent and should be changed to "warm," which they felt would be less frightening to the children reading the book. Of course, Sendak refused. As he explained, the whole point of the book is emotional heat. Sendak believed that children were tuned in to a higher frequency of emotion than adults; the happiness of adults is elation in a child, and anger their rage. The monsters (which Sendak modeled after his aunts and uncles) are the embodiment of Max's rage. He enters their realm bubbling over with anger toward his mother and the world. It is only when Max leaves the monsters behind that he can return home to a new kind of heat: the comfort of a home-cooked meal and the company of his mother.

CAT'S CRADLE
Kurt Vonnegut
-
1963

If I were a younger man, I would write a history of human stupidity; and I would climb to the top of Mount McCabe and lie down on my back with my history for a pillow; and I would take from the ground some of the blue-white poison that makes statues of men; and I would make a statue of myself, lying on my back, grinning horribly, and thumbing my nose at You Know Who.

It is no surprise that the end of Kurt Vonnegut's fourth novel is equal parts funny and bleak; he is, after all, a master of dark comedy. The snide sentiment belongs to the practical and cynical Bokonon, whose pragmatism appears to have broken down at last following the apocalypse ignited by the accidental, but completely predictable, release of ice-nine (the "blue-white poison" he refers to, an alternative structure of water that is solid at room temperature). Instead of using Bokonism, the religion he created, to push through this latest setback, Bokonon feels that the incredible shortsightedness that led to it deserves to be remembered, which he is willing to give his own life in order to ensure.

THE BELL JAR
Sylvia Plath
-
1963

The eyes and faces all turned themselves towards me, and guiding myself by them, as by a magical thread, I stepped into the room.

The Bell Jar, the poet Sylvia Plath's only novel, is semi-autobiographical, with parts inspired by Plath's long battle with clinical depression and bipolar disorder. Since Plath took her own life less than a month after the book's publication, the book's title has become shorthand for that struggle, particularly when it appears in young women. Due to her dark mental state, Plath's alter ego, Esther Greenwood, suffers through her life despite gaining an opportunity at a prestigious magazine in New York. When the big city, job, and peers fail to free her from the jar's confines, she makes an earnest suicide attempt (after making several half-hearted ones) by swallowing sleeping pills. The attempt fails and Esther is committed to a mental hospital, where she is subjected to electric shock treatment and discovers the jar that has been suffocating her. Envious of the agency men are allowed in society and terrified by her own fragile condition, Esther does make a turn toward improvement toward the novel's close, becoming less and less oppressed by her fear. She is finally able to guide herself, rather than be guided by the expectations of others, and confidently step from the jar into a new realm.

CITY OF NIGHT
John Rechy
-
1963

And the fierce wind is an echo of angry childhood and of a very scared boy looking out the window— remembering my dead dog outside by the wounded house as the gray Texas dust gradually covered her up—and thinking: It isn't fair! Why cant dogs go to Heaven?

In his debut novel *City of Night*, John Rechy describes the life of a gay sex worker trying to make his way in 1960s America. Considered one of the first published works to deal with "the homosexual underground," this novel found a home in the burgeoning countercultural movement of its time. Rechy, who himself is a gay man with experience as a sex worker in Times Square, modeled many aspects of the unnamed protagonist after himself, including setting the final scene in Texas, where Rechy grew up.

A CONFEDERATE GENERAL FROM BIG SUR

Richard Brautigan

-

1964

Then there are more and more endings: the sixth, the 53rd, the 131st, the 9,435th ending, endings going faster and faster, more and more endings, faster and faster until this book is having 186,000 endings per second.

Richard Brautigan's first novel, *A Confederate General from Big Sur*, was largely ignored upon its initial release, likely because of its focus on countercultural themes such as dropping out of society and creating one's own reality. Ironically, *A Confederate General from Big Sur* is actually a critique of the untraditional approach it seems to celebrate, since its meandering prose and pointless plot show the dangers of leading a disorganized life. Such an existence can never truly find a satisfactory resolution, the dizzying horror of which Brautigan captures in the novel's close.

151

SECOND SKIN

John Hawkes

-

1964

That's it. The sun in the evening. The moon at dawn.
The still voice.

John Hawkes once said, "I began to write fiction on the
assumption that the true enemies of the novel were plot,
character, setting and theme." It may seem impossible for a
novelist to avoid these four elements, but that did not stop
Hawkes from trying. *Second Skin* tells the story of Skipper, an
ex–World War II naval lieutenant who has survived despite
encountering considerable hardships and tragedies. The story
is a told in a nonlinear fashion through a series of flashbacks,
which subverts a plot's expected manner of unfolding and
makes it difficult for the reader to get a handle on the characters'
identities and motivations. The setting Skipper is narrating
from is vaguely described as an island, and it is unclear if the
events Skipper describes are real or imagined. In the hands
of a lesser writer, these approaches could make for a mess of
a book, but Hawkes writes masterfully, evoking beauty while
describing horrible events, arousing empathy in moments that
seem entirely unsympathetic. While he was not able to fully
conquer his enemies in this novel, he did manage to make the
known world seem entirely new.

A MOVEABLE FEAST

Ernest Hemingway

-

1964

But this is how Paris was in the early days when we were very poor and very happy.

Published posthumously, Ernest Hemingway's memoir *A Moveable Feast* is about his coming of age in 1920s Paris. Started after recovering some notebooks that had been stored in the basement of the Hotel Ritz Paris, Hemingway's lyrical depiction creates a painfully romantic picture of the great city—painful because those who fall under Hemingway's spell will go to find the city completely changed. That time was before Hemingway was an icon, but his zeal for the good things in life makes his future status as a literary star seem all but assured. Yet one cannot help but wonder if the great Hemingway, who took his life a year after finishing his memoir, would have been better off if he'd remained very poor and relatively unknown.

STONER
John Williams
-
1965

The fingers loosened, and the book they had held moved slowly and then swiftly across the still body and fell into the silence of the room.

Initially published in 1965, John Williams's *Stoner* went out of print just a year later due to poor sales. However, after its republication in 2003 and the chiming in of a handful of influential voices, including the *New Yorker*, sales skyrocketed. The book's success, however, came far too late for the author, who died in 1994. The series of events surrounding the book's initial flop ironically mirror the career of the protagonist, William Stoner. William is a hardworking college professor who cares deeply about his job, yet it seems that he is unable to succeed no matter what. His marriage satisfies neither him nor his wife, the college at which he teaches remains antagonistic toward him after he fails a senior professor's favorite student, and the one thing that seems to bring him joy, an affair with a younger teacher, is brought to an abrupt end by the faculty. In the end, William dies alone, gripping the one, unsuccessful book he published in his lifetime. While the ending is pretty depressing, there is a modicum of hope: while William has passed on, his book remains, carrying on his legacy.

CASTLE KEEP
William Eastlake
-
1965

We had the castle within us. We carried it away.

Set at a historic castle in Belgium, William Eastlake's *Castle Keep* tells the story of an American company of soldiers assigned to defend an ancient castle and the artifacts within. As the men wait out the war, expecting to be attacked at any moment, they wonder why such a thing is worth the life of a man. Places, after all, can be rebuilt, can't they? Over time, however, the eclectic group of soldiers grows attached to the historic place and its inhabitants, and by the time the Germans strike, they are fighting as much for the fortress as they are for their lives. In the end, the castle goes down. But it is not destroyed, as the soldiers carry their love and all it taught them away.

THE CRYING OF LOT 49
Thomas Pynchon

-

1966

Oedipa settled back, to await the crying of lot 49.

The Crying of Lot 49 ends with Oedipa Maas on the verge of resolving the byzantine mystery she became embroiled in when she discovered that she was named executrix of her former lover Pierce Inverarity's will. This opportunity leads Oedipa to discover the possible existence of a secretive underground postal delivery service known as the Trystero. Although, it might just be an elaborate prank that her former beau has decided to play on her. In her effort to unravel the potential conspiracy, she comes upon a group of eccentrics who shine underneath the light of Thomas Pynchon's hyper-sarcastic wit. At the end, Oedipa is at an auction where she suspects that representatives of the Trystero are waiting to bid on a set of rare postage stamps, but we do not discover the result, for in this novel there can be no satisfying resolution.

GILES GOAT-BOY
John Barth
-
1966

Nonetheless I smiled, leaned on my stick, and, no troubleder than Mom, gimped in to meet the guards halfway.

John Barth claimed that *Giles Goat-Boy* was "the first American postmodernist novel." And while that bold claim has been disputed frequently, there is no argument over the novel being postmodern, as the book is absurd, encyclopedic, and highly self-conscious. Chronicling the journey of George Giles, a human who was raised as a goat and goes on to consider himself the messiah, the story is rife with allusions to religion, mythology, and philosophy, and has been seen as an allegory of both the Cold War and the hero's journey described by Joseph Campbell in *The Hero with a Thousand Faces*. The story takes place on the campus of New Tammany College (a campus which encompasses the entire universe), where Giles constructs his heroic identity and rises to become the Grand Tutor, or spiritual leader. By the end he has fulfilled his destiny, but pushes on, just as his heroic path demands.

IN COLD BLOOD
Truman Capote

-

1966

Then starting home, he walked toward the trees, and under them, leaving behind him the big sky, the whisper of wind voices in the wind-bent wheat.

Considered by many to be the first book of true crime, Truman Capote's wildly popular *In Cold Blood* uses elements of fiction to explore a real event. After reading about the murder of the Clutter family in Holcomb, Kansas, Capote and his good friend Harper Lee traveled to the small rural town to conduct research for a story in *The New Yorker*. Upon meeting with the two men who had been convicted of the murders, Richard Hickock and Perry Smith, it became clear to Capote that this was a rare opportunity to see evil up close. Once provided with this opportunity, a surprisingly nuanced truth arose: that these men, particularly Smith, may be deserving of sympathy despite their horrific actions. In the end, lawman Alvin Dewey walks through a cemetery and reflects on the recent execution of the two killers, the tragedy they caused, and how that act has haunted and changed the small town he is charged with watching over.

WHY ARE WE IN VIETNAM?
Norman Mailer
-
1967

Vietnam, hot dam.

Norman Mailer's novel *Why Are We in Vietnam?* is narrated by D.J., a young man who is about to be sent to fight in Vietnam. The hunting trip he recounts to the reader, however, occurs approximately two years before he is drafted. The trip takes place in Alaska, where D.J., his best friend Tex, and their fathers go in the hopes of killing a grizzly bear. The overbearing Texan masculinity of the boys' fathers is constantly undermined by D.J.'s commentary on the unfair advantage the hunter has. After watching his father bag a grizzly, D.J. becomes wholly suspicious of the group's motivations and heads into the wilderness with his friend—and without any supplies. The experience the two have connects them to nature in a way previously unavailable during their attempts to control it with technology, and one has the sense that regardless of what happens in Vietnam, the peace that this moment has brought will serve D.J. well.

SNOW WHITE
Donald Barthelme

-

1967

THE HEROES DEPART IN SEARCH OF A NEW PRINCIPLE HEIGH-HO

The fairy tale, like the fable or parable, is accessible by design. The reader is supposed to digest the contents easily, and the structure is typically predictable. What happens, though, when you turn these simple stories on their head? Donald Barthelme does just that in *Snow White*, reconstructing the classic tale to examine the concessions and decisions the characters have to make, as well as their own identities. What results is a far more adult, thought-provoking version. At the novel's end Barthelme puts his own spin on the obvious takeaways and interpretations that attend these stories, breaking down his complex construction and presenting the reader with a list of interpretations they can tidily store away.

TROUT FISHING IN AMERICA
Richard Brautigan
-
1967

P.S.

Sorry I forgot to give you the mayonnaise.

Richard Brautigan's *Trout Fishing in America* is a cult classic, despite the author's efforts to prevent that classification. The extremely self-aware work lacks a storyline, character arcs, and every other element of a novel, besides words. To give you an idea, the first chapter of the book is a discussion of the book's cover, which is a photo of Brautigan. "Trout Fishing in America" is not only the book's title, it is used as the name of a character and a hotel, used to describe the act of fishing itself, and even used as a modifier. This surreal approach allowed Brautigan to fire away incessantly at the mainstream, and his comic, irreverent takes were so well received that, for a time, he and his unorthodox novel seemed destined to end up there.

ONE HUNDRED YEARS
OF SOLITUDE

Gabriel García Márquez

-

1967

Before reaching the final line, however, he had already understood that he would never leave that room, for it was foreseen that the city of mirrors (or mirages) would be wiped out by the wind and exiled from the memory of men at the precise moment when Aureliano Babilonia would finish deciphering the parchments, and that everything written on them was unrepeatable since time immemorial and forever more, because races condemned to one hundred years of solitude did not have a second opportunity on earth.

Few novels are more beloved than *One Hundred Years of Solitude*. William Kennedy, a great writer in his own right, said this in his review of the novel for the *New York Times*: "*One Hundred Years of Solitude* is the first piece of literature since the Book of Genesis that should be required reading for the entire human race. Mr. García Márquez has done nothing less than to create in the reader a sense of all that is profound, meaningful, and meaningless in life." To close out a book that possesses this kind of force is no easy feat, but Márquez is up to the task. Instead of settling for a tidy resolution, Márquez wipes his creation out of existence. As the last Buendía, Aureliano, reads a prophecy that depicts every misfortune that befell his family, he sees that the town in which they'd lived is about to be destroyed by a hurricane. Talk about final.

WILLIE MASTERS' LONESOME WIFE
William H. Gass
-
1968

YOU HAVE FALLEN INTO ART – RETURN TO LIFE

The specific font and typographic treatment of the final line in William Gass's *Willie Masters' Lonesome Wife* are just as important as the words. The book includes innovative variations on traditional text blocks, accompanied by photos of a nude woman. The nude pictures, along with the erotic passages, are meant to examine the sexual relationship between a man and woman, specifically Babs Masters and a man named Gelvin, while the captivating structure examines the relationship between the reader and text. By drawing attention to these two separate associations, Gass seems to be saying that they are quite similar, with each relying on one individual becoming entranced.

THE UNIVERSAL BASEBALL ASSOCIATION, INC., J. HENRY WAUGH, PROP.

Robert Coover

-

1968

"Hang loose," he says, and pulling down his mask, trots back behind home plate.

J. Henry Waugh, the protagonist of Robert Coover's *The Universal Baseball Association, Inc., J. Henry Waugh, Prop.*, tolerates the events of everyday life, knowing that at the end of the day he will return to his apartment and enter the world of the Universal Baseball Association: a league of his invention where every outcome is determined by rolling dice. When the imaginary rookie, Damon Rutherford, pitches a perfect game, Henry begins to push his luck. Soon the godlike role that Henry plays becomes more severe and he demands more from his players. After the death of his star pitcher due to a string of bad rolls, Henry falls into a bout of depression. Eventually, he breaks his own personal code and manipulates the rules of the game in order to kill the pitcher responsible for the rookie's death. In the final chapter, we see through the eyes of Henry's imaginary players as they gather together, mourning the death of their friend and fellow player. While one of them suggests that there may be some higher power exercising influence over their daily lives, the end of the novel leaves that topic to the thinkers of their world. As for the players, they simply exist to play ball.

A FAN'S NOTES
Frederick Exley
-
1968

And when again the vision comes, I find that, ready to do battle, I am running: obsessively running.

A self-proclaimed "fictional memoir," Frederick Exley's *A Fan's Note* is an account of his own life interspersed with elements of fantasy. Half obsessive love letter to New York Giants running back Frank Gifford, half ruminations on a life marred by mental illness and crippling alcoholism, the novel examines the decay of the American Dream. As the book follows Exley through failure, success, institutionalization, and love, he constantly views his own life in relation to his hero. Gifford, a handsome, rugged, powerful man who embodies the American ideal, casts a long shadow of inadequacy over Exley's life. Exley fears that he is doomed to be nothing more than a fan, both in sports and in his life, a man who is never satisfied with himself.

FAT CITY
Leonard Gardner
-
1969

*He came lightly down the metal steps into balmy air
and diesel fumes, and feeling in himself the potent
allegiance of fate, he pushed open the door to the lobby,
where unkempt sleepers slumped upright on
the benches.*

Fat City, Leonard Gardner's first and only novel, tells the story
of two boxers: Billy Tully, a washed-up boxer sickened by a
string of defeats who hopes to come out of retirement to restore
his legacy, and Ernie Munger, a kid with a ton of potential but
no direction. Their lives run along simultaneously, Billy failing
to reclaim his past glory and ending up back on a barstool;
Ernie trying desperately to hold on to his talents as he feels his
promising future slipping away. In the end, Billy gives up on his
dream of a comeback and settles into a life of quiet alcoholism
and solemn reflection. In the closing line, Ernie stumbles off
a Greyhound bus at night and walks among the bus station
regulars. Surrounded by people who belong nowhere, we can
tell Ernie has not yet given up completely, but we can feel the
doubt tugging at him.

THEM

Joyce Carol Oates

–

1969

He took his sister's hand and kissed it and said good-by, making an ironic, affectionate bow over her with his head; it was the Jules she had always loved, and now she loved him for going away, saying good-by, leaving her forever.

Joyce Carol Oates once said she is happy that of all her stories, *Them* is what she'll most be remembered for. It tells the story of a struggling American family in Detroit. Loretta, her son, Jules, and her daughter, Maureen, are the central characters of the novel. As situations become increasingly tough, each character abandons restraint, and, one by one, turns to crime in order to survive. By the end of the novel, the siblings' lives diverge: Maureen starts a family and turns her life around. Jules, however, does not. He becomes increasingly more selfish and commits far worse crimes, eventually raping a woman and murdering a man. In the end, a defeated Jules visits Maureen, who is expecting a child. He tells her he is running away to California, and although she does not say it explicitly, Maureen knows that she will never see Jules again. The last line gives a clear depiction of two separate paths one can take out of poverty: one tragic, and the other uplifting and hopeful.

BULLET PARK

John Cheever

-

1969

Tony went back to school on Monday and Nailles—drugged—went off to work and everything was as wonderful, wonderful, wonderful, wonderful as it had been.

The suburban world of *Bullet Park* has gone horribly wrong, and the only thing that can set it right is a sacrifice. At least, that is what Paul Hammer thinks. A man fueled by alcohol, neurosis, and the dying words of his insane mother, Hammer chooses Tony Nailles as his target. Both Tony and his father, Eliot, suffer from depression. They each treat their depression differently: Tony with mindless activities, like sleeping and watching television, Eliot with tranquilizers.

Hammer believes that by burning Tony on the church altar like a biblical prophet, he can save the inhabitants of Bullet Park from their own ennui. Fortunately, Eliot foils the plot of the deranged Hammer and rescues his son. The Nailles family is free to return to their mundane, predictable suburban existence once more. Saved from its possible redemption, America is free to continue along, drugged and untroubled by the crushing despair it contains.

THE BAMBOO BED
William Eastlake
-
1969

There was death—she was our captain's bride.

Written after William Eastlake's service as a war reporter during the Vietnam War, *The Bamboo Bed* fully exposes the insanity and horror of the jungle. The novel's protagonists, Captain Clancy and Captain Knightbridge, are both stationed in Vietnam. While Clancy lies dying on a bamboo bed thousands of miles away from his home, Knightbridge sails above the jungle in his helicopter, aptly named *The Bamboo Bed*, performing rescue missions and personal liaisons amid the chaos. Clancy spends his final days on his bamboo bed in a hallucination-filled stupor, discussing philosophy with a snake and a tiger—creatures who belong in the jungle, unlike himself. The book ends with Knightbridge attempting a rescue mission to pick up injured soldiers. Flying into a powerful storm, *The Bamboo Bed* plunges into the jungle below, where only thing left is death.

THE FRENCH LIEUTENANT'S WOMAN

John Fowles

-

1969

*And out again, upon the unplumb'd, salt,
estranging sea.*

In John Fowles's *The French Lieutenant's Woman*, the reader alone gets to choose how the novel will end. Sarah Woodruff and Charles Smithson are the main characters of this postmodern work. Abandoned by a French ship's officer and written off by her town as a "tragedy," Sarah has lived a hard life full of rejection and disgrace. Charles, meanwhile, is a man of high social and financial standing who is engaged to a woman named Ernestina, the daughter of a wealthy tradesman. Upon seeing Sarah, Charles becomes infatuated with her and suggests that she leave town so he is not tempted by her presence. She obliges. The narrator, represented as a physical character, in postmodern fashion, gives the reader three possible endings for the couple. In the first, the two never meet again, and Sarah's fate is left unknown. In the second, Sarah and Charles have an affair and Charles proposes to her in a letter that never arrives. They reunite two years later and Sarah introduces Charles to his child, a result of their affair. The third ending is the same as the second, except that Charles expresses no interest in the child and feels Sarah manipulated him. In all endings, Charles comes to the conclusion that life is a raging sea of choices, so we must actively push to create our own destiny.

SLAUGHTERHOUSE-FIVE
Kurt Vonnegut
-
1969

One bird said to Billy Pilgrim, "Poo-tee-weet?"

In the introduction to *Slaughterhouse-Five*, Kurt Vonnegut writes that he considers his novel to be largely unsuccessful, "because there is nothing intelligent to say about a massacre." Centered around the senseless bombing of Dresden during World War II, *Slaughterhouse-Five* follows the story of Billy Pilgrim, a survivor of the bombing who goes on to travel through time and space, eventually experiencing all of time simultaneously for eternity. Through the science-fiction absurdity of Pilgrim's life, the reader is reminded of the sheer incommunicable nature of human tragedy through the repeated line "So it goes." Ending with Pilgrim back at the time of the Dresden bombing, the book chooses to focus our attention to the simple beauty of a birdsong instead of the indescribable tragedy behind him, a callback to Vonnegut's belief that there is nothing intelligent to say about a massacre.

JEREMIAH 8:20
Carol DeChellis Hill
-
1970

... He could see the country, hear the country get it all at last and so the new god rolled speeding through the nights, the clouds darkening once over Kansas, the wind rising slowly he rolled speeding through the country and the waste, sometimes people awoke thinking they had heard a heartbeat in the night, and it did not stop the electronic bike until outside Kansas City on Route 22 when folks said a terrible noise went up a flash split across the sky like nothing they could remember.

Jeremiah Francis Scanlon, the protagonist of Carol DeChellis Hill's debut novel *Jeremiah 8:20*, is an overweight man in his mid-30s. Stuck in a dead-end job and increasingly baffled by the world as he grows older, Jeremiah is an unlikely main character who straddles the line between bumbling stupidity and sympathetic naivety as he blindly stumbles his way through life. Convinced that the black community holds the answers to life's secrets, Jeremiah purchases a tape recorder and eavesdrops on as many people's conversations as he can. Embarking on a journey of misguided discovery, he travels across America on a motorcycle, recording cardiac arrests, suicides, and dreams of demons along the way. The last lines hold a certain amount of unsettling jubilation as Francis maniacally tries to understand the human experience and himself as he drives across the country, preparing for the biblical harvest alluded to in the title verse.

ANOTHER ROADSIDE ATTRACTION

Tom Robbins

-

1971

Let Amanda be your pine cone.

Tom Robins re-creates the feeling of the '60s in his novel *Another Roadside Attraction*. The novel tells the story of Amanda, her husband, John Paul Ziller, and their baboon, Mon Cul, who is the only living thing to know of a rhyme for orange. They invest in a new business venture: a roadside attraction featuring a hot dog stand and a makeshift zoo. Marx Marvelous, a character with a background as ridiculous as his name, infiltrates the roadside zoo under the guise of a zoo manager in order to research the 1960s counterculture movement for secret agents in Washington. In a story that never fully leaves absurdity, the protagonists reconnect with their old friend Westminster "Plucky" Purcell, who ends up stealing the bones of Jesus Christ from the Vatican and stashing them in an exhibit at their roadside stand. Forced to part ways under the threat of Vatican monks proficient in unarmed combat, the protagonists separate. In the end, the reader is left with only Amanda and her unassuming spirituality to guide them through the bizarre haze of the '60s.

GRENDEL
John Gardner
-
1971

"Poor Grendel's had an accident," I whisper. "So may you all."

Taking place in the same universe as the epic poem *Beowulf*, John Gardner's novel *Grendel* details the 12 years before Beowulf goes to Hrothgar's Hall. By exploring Grendel as more than a one-dimensional monster, at its core, *Grendel* is a book about perspective. Grendel, struggling to find his place in a world of humans who spite him at every turn, morphs from villain to antihero as the story progresses. Driven to destroy humanity yet enchanted by their ability to tell stories and sing, Grendel becomes increasingly more conflicted about his place in the universe. In the final chapter, Grendel faces off against Beowulf in a retelling of their legendary fight that paints

Beowulf as an impressive but cruel fighter, unconcerned with honor. Wounded and dying, Grendel runs back to the entrance of his cave, cursing the ignorant animals that surround him to a similar fate at the hands of the brutal humans.

DOUBLE OR NOTHING

Raymond Federman

-

1971

Then it does not necessarily have to be NOODLES!

Best described as a visual object novel, Raymond Federman's work of metafiction *Double or Nothing* tells two simultaneous stories at once: the first is of a man trying desperately to write a story; the other focuses on the plot of the story being written. No two pages in Federman's novel are laid out quite the same, meaning how things are shown are as important as what is being said on the page. The stories overlap as the narrator struggles with minute decisions like the prices of various household goods. Rife with indecision, the narrator's tiny changes cause ripple effects through the story and everything starts over again. The ending line suggests that the story will never be finished: the narrator will never "double down" and instead will continue to fret over every decision until he loses the story entirely through his lack of commitment and constant changes.

WATERSHIP DOWN
Richard Adams
-
1972

He reached the top of the bank in a single, powerful leap. Hazel followed; and together they slipped away, running easily down through the wood, where the first primroses were beginning to bloom.

Richard Adams's *Watership Down* follows a warren of anthropomorphized rabbits on their journey for survival. Fiver, a seer rabbit, attempts to warn his fellow warren members about the imminent destruction of their home. Barely escaping the warren with their lives, the remaining rabbits elect Hazel, Fiver's brother, as the leader of their search for a new home. Battling rabbits and humans alike, this story bridges the gap between children's fable and survival novel. After dozens of near-death experiences and a final battle with the neighboring warren, Hazel successfully ensures the survival of their new home in Watership Down. In the final lines, Hazel crosses over to the afterlife and is approached by El-ahrairah, the mythological hero of all rabbits, who invites Hazel to join his elite guard. Even in his death, Hazel ensures the survival of his people and retires to a land free from humans and their bloodshed.

DAUGHTER BUFFALO
Janet Frame
-
1972

What matters is that I have what I gave; nothing is completely taken; we meet in the common meeting place in the calm of stone, the frozen murmurs of life, squamata, sauria, serpentes; *in the sanctuary.*

The only novel New Zealand's Janet Frame set in America, *Daughter Buffalo* focuses on the unique ways Western civilizations deal with death. Talbot Edelman, one of the book's two narrators, is a medical student in New York City who is fascinated by death. The second narrator, Turnlung, is an aging poet from the Southern Hemisphere fascinated by America's obsession with dying. Convinced of the inseparable nature of life and death, the two "adopt" a baby buffalo from the local zoo. Turnlung refers to the animal as his "death-jewel," linking the value of life to the precious nature of death. After Turnlung's death, we see him in the vast, open prarie of the afterlife with his buffalo by his side, free to enjoy nature uninhibited by Western society. Turnlung suggests that, like the reptiles in his ending line, perhaps death allows us, too, to shed our pasts and grow anew.

ALL MY FRIENDS ARE GOING TO BE STRANGERS

Larry McMurtry

-

1972

"I had rather go see the rivers," I said, but I don't know if he heard me and if he did he wouldn't have understood, he was too normal to understand, if my friends came and asked him why I had left he wouldn't know, he had never stood in the river, I don't think he swirled as I was swirling, he didn't seem to yearn to flow, he didn't much want to be undertaken, he didn't remember Zapata and hadn't even read the great Juan de la Cosa, and if they came, my friends, if Wu came, for some reason, or Godwin, or Jenny, they wouldn't get it from him, he wouldn't know why I loved the river, why I loved any of the people I loved, they wouldn't get it from him and none of them could guess, only maybe Jill could, I knew only Jill could, if I had stayed, if she had stayed, I could tell her, she might guess, she had the clearest eyes, the straightest look, the most honest face, I missed it so—but ah no, no chance, better to just want rivers—Jill was gone.

In Larry McMurtry's novel *All My Friends Are Going to Be*

Strangers, the protagonist, Danny Deck, is in between lives. From a small-town Texas boy to a big shot writer in Hollywood, Danny's life is surrounded by love, loss, and frustration. After a failed marriage and the sudden publication of his book by Random House, Danny finds himself isolated from his friends and family and falls into an existential crisis. While writing his second novel in Hollywood, he meets Jill. The two start a relationship together, one that holds through most of the novel despite the lovers' burned-out state. In the last portion of the book, Jill breaks up with Danny over the phone, leading him to wade into the Rio Grande to try and drown his latest manuscript. The final lines show Danny's isolation as he desperately tries to trade his success for his old life and friends.

G.

John Berger

-

1972

The horizon is the straight bottom edge of a curtain arbitrarily and suddenly lowered upon a performance.

Considered a spiritual successor to *Don Juan* and *Casanova*, John Berger's *G.* follows the escapades of the son of an Italian canned fruit merchant as he seeks to build an identity through promiscuous sex. Abandoned by his parents early on and seduced by a female relative at the age of 14, G. floats through life disconnected from the world, moving from one female conquest to another in a fleeting attempt to create some meaning in his life. The book follows a postmodernist structure, including stream-of-consciousness passages that follow the apathetic G. up to the historical events of the Milan worker riots of 1898. In a unique moment of interest in the world outside of his desires, G. joins the angry mob of workers and is quickly beaten to death. The curtain of the horizon drops over the sordid life of G. as he falls below the surface of the water, leaving behind no real accomplishments to remember him by.

SULA

Toni Morrison

-

1973

It was a fine cry—loud and long—but it had no bottom and it had no top, just circles and circles of sorrow.

Toni Morrison brings to life the impoverished residents of the town of Bottom in her novel *Sula*. The main characters, Nel and Sula, are as complementary as they are different. Nel, the local Goody Two-Shoes, lives in a restrictive family that pushes her toward traditional stability. Sula, on the other hand, is a wild card, defying gender roles and societal expectations. Sula acts on her own desires, leaving Bottom after high school and engaging in multiple affairs. Nel's life follows a more traditional path. She settles down and marries Jude, another resident of Bottom. Ten years later, Sula returns to Bottom and carries out an affair with Jude, shattering her friendship with Nel. Only when Sula is on her deathbed do the two finally reconcile. After Sula's death, Nel realizes that Sula's wildness helped keep Bottom alive. While it is unclear if she forgives Sula fully for her actions, she mourns the loss of her friend and the eventual end of Bottom in the closing line.

CRASH
J. G. Ballard
-
1973

The aircraft rise from the runways of the airport, carrying the remnants of Vaughan's semen to the instrument panels and radiator grilles of a thousand crashing cars, the leg stances of a million passengers.

J. G. Ballard's novel *Crash* explores the prevalence of automobiles in human interaction through a pornographic obsession with automotive crashes. Vaughan, a stalker-sadist, seeks out the sites of various car crashes to perform sexual acts on the wreckage. The main characters soon find themselves increasingly drawn to the sites of violent car crashes, first out of morbid curiosity and later for stimulation. Their sexualities become so entangled with the presence of the mechanical that they can no longer find enjoyment without the violent presence of the machines. The opening line of the novel tells us that Vaughan dies in a car crash. In an unassuming tie-in to the final lines, we see an aircraft take off from the site of Vaughan's last crash as his body is irrevocably mingled with millions of roadway passengers and the machines they've come to depend on.

OUT
Ronald Sukenick
-
1973

---

this way this way this way this way this way this way this

way out this

way out

O

A prime example of innovative fiction, Ronald Sukenick's *Out* is violent in both content and design, employing a gradual decay until the text is surrounded in white space. The narrator, Carl, who takes on other names as he travels, brings the reader through a series of seemingly unrelated sequences ranging from organized criminals lining the ledge of a building with sticks of dynamite clenched in their teeth, to spiritual advice from the Empty Fox on the fragility of existence. Much like a cloud, the plot of *Out* seems to change with each page, condensing the chaos of urbanization and political culture until it weighs heavily and incomprehensibly over the reader. In the last line, we are left following the narrator in a desperate scramble to find our way out of both modernity and the novel.

GRAVITY'S RAINBOW
Thomas Pynchon
-
1973

Now everybody—

Thomas Pynchon's *Gravity's Rainbow* dwells on the paranoia surrounding war and the effects of psychological conditioning on the psyche. A mix of literary fiction and metaphysical speculation, this book explores the erratic behaviors of individuals as they seek an explanation for the horrors of war. Loosely centered around Pirate Prentice and his search for

Rocket 00000, a part-machine, part-man program that defies all conventional naming systems, the exploits of the book become increasingly removed from reality as the novel spirals inward, eventually ending in a theater just before a missile strike. The last lines seem to encourage the reader to join in the chaos prior to everything being consumed by the miasma of war.

MRS. OCTOBER WAS HERE
Coleman Dowell
-
1974

Fin. Fin?

Mrs. October, the central character of Coleman Dowell's *Mrs. October Was Here*, is a revolutionary with one goal in mind: to eradicate hatred. She hopes to accomplish this monumental feat simply by writing down her wishes, which in turn makes them come true. The power that Mrs. October's writing has over people, while at first effectively enacting change, eventually leads to her becoming a prophet who rules over the fictional town of Tasmania, Ohio. Pained by her legacy, Mrs. October stages her own voluntary crucifixion. The final page, marked by the classic "Fin," is followed up with a question. Perhaps, though Mrs. October has perished, her revolution has not.

THE LAST DAYS OF LOUISIANA RED

Ishmael Reed

-

1974

ZOO ATTENDANT'S SKULL FRACTURED: BABOON CHARGED.

Louisiana Red, the corporation at the center of Ishmael Reed's *The Last Days of Louisiana Red*, represents all that is bad in the world. The corporation, headed by a witch named Marie, specializes in highly addictive drugs created to oppress black Americans. The only one who can take down the industry is Ed Yellings, owner and operator of Solid Gumbo Works.

When Yellings is found dead, in comes Papa LaBas, a detective who takes it upon himself to solve the case after hearing of Yellings from a talking baboon at the zoo. As the plot unfolds, it becomes clear Yellings was murdered because he was on the cusp of discovering a cure to heroin addiction, a discovery which would cripple Louisiana Red's industry. As LaBas sits contently on the plane home, having unraveled the complex thicket of a mystery to the best of anyone's ability, he notices an interesting newspaper headline. It seems that Yellings wasn't the only one tired of being exploited.

THE HAIR OF HAROLD ROUX
Thomas Williams

-

1974

The brave, eternal angle of her hip as she stands, in a light dress, melts his heart and he holds out his arms to her.

Aaron Benham, the aging New England protagonist of Thomas Williams's *The Hair of Harold Roux*, is a writer and professor who is on leave from university to finish his novel. The narrative takes the form of multiple stories intercutting Aaron's own life, including the plot of his manuscript, also called *The Hair of Harold Roux*, and the narrative of a fairy tale he once told his children. Aaron's novel, based off of his time at college after World War II, follows Allard Benson, a fictional foil of Aaron himself, as he destroys his relationship with his closest friend and the two women he loves. In reality, Aaron watches himself making the same mistakes as his character as he fails to help his friend George keep his job and fantasizes of an affair with George's wife. In the closing image, Aaron dreams of a perfect woman: an amalgamation of all the women he has loved. He reaches out to her, welcoming the fantasy over his reality.

THE EBONY TOWER

John Fowles

-

1974

They disappear among the poplars. The meadow is empty. The river, the meadow, the cliff and cloud. The princess calls, but there is no one, now, to hear her.

John Fowles's *The Ebony Tower* is comprised of five short novellas that contain interwoven themes and characters. Beginning with the story of Henry Breasley, a painter who lives with two of his female former art students. Henry's retirement is interrupted by David, an artist attempting to create Henry's biography. As the volumes progress, the initial story begins to distort, echoing its way through each of the remaining volumes until the final story. The fifth section, titled "The Cloud," is a convoluted, fragmented narrative that describes a group of family and friends on a picnic. Some of the characters from the earlier sections can be found here, but their narrative is not linear. In a callback to Henry's career as a painter, the picnicgoers are described as enclosed in the scene, like a painting. As the characters leave us one by one, we are left with only the faintest of echoes of the prior story in the landscape as the princess is left behind. Like Henry, she is unable to escape.

RUMBLE FISH

S. E. Hinton

-

1975

I figured if I didn't see, I'd start forgetting again. But it's been taking me longer than I thought it would.

The rockabilly, leather jackets, motorcycles, and muscle cars of 1960s American greaser gangs were long gone by the time S. E. Hinton wrote *Rumble Fish*, and perhaps that was the point. Rusty-James, the protagonist, runs into Steve, his childhood best friend. Fresh out of the reformatory, Rusty-James recalls the events that led up to his incarceration, including a knife fight with the local bully, Biff. Rusty-James's brother, known only as Motorcycle Boy, has returned home from California, and saves the boys from the knife fight, as well as a back-alley mugging. Near the end of the novel, Motorcycle Boy and Rusty-James stand in front of a tank of Siamese fighting fish, wondering if the fish would behave as violently if they were free. Motorcycle Boy breaks into the pet store and steals the fish to release them into the river. He is shot on sight by a police officer, killing both him and the fish. In the last lines, Rusty-James decides to avoid seeing Steve again, as Steve reminds him of his own tangled past. Like the fish, Rusty-James feels cornered, trapped in a world where violence is the only option.

RAGTIME

E. L. Doctorow

-

1975

And Harry K. Thaw, having obtained his release from the insane asylum, marched annually at Newport in the Armistice Day parade.

The main characters in E. L. Doctorow's historical novel *Ragtime* serve as tour guides to the racial and societal tensions of early 20th-century America. Named only by their position in the family, these main characters act as a backdrop for a revolving cast of characters and historical figures alike. Coalhouse Walker Jr., the lover and fiancé of the family's maid, Sarah, becomes the central focus halfway through the novel, as his car is defaced in a racist display by the local fire department. Coalhouse argues against his treatment and is thrown in prison. He is bailed out by the family. Coalhouse, in an act of defiance, fills J. P. Morgan's abandoned mansion and library with dynamite and holds it hostage in exchange for safe passage and the restoration of his car. The police agree, but Coalhouse is shot on sight as he leaves the building. The final lines move away from Coalhouse and the family as we see Harry K. Thaw, a white man institutionalized for the killing of Stanford White and accused of sexually assaulting actress Evelyn Nesbit, free to celebrate the American war effort, unpunished for his crimes.

J R

William Gaddis

-

1975

*So I mean listen I got this neat idea hey, you
listening? Hey? You listening...?*

William Gaddis never wanted his readers to think too hard
while reading *J R*, his satirical novel about the American
Dream. Conveyed entirely in disjointed, unattributed dialogue
that never pauses long enough to listen, *J R* tells the story of an
11-year-old latchkey kid of the same name who builds a corporate
empire from his school's pay phone. As *J R*'s fabricated business
grows, it swallows the lives and dreams of his employees and
partners with it, most notably those of his former music teacher
Mr Bast, who downgrades his goal of penning an opera to help
J R with his stock scheme. In the end, we are left with a novel
that illustrates the hollowness of corporate America and shows
how unchecked greed slowly destroys everything in its path. In
the final lines, the story continues to another business scheme
as the characters once again try and center the attention onto
themselves instead of listening to those around them.

A TOMB FOR
BORIS DAVIDOVICH
Danilo Kiš

-

1976

*Darmolatov's case was entered in all the latest
pathology textbooks. A photograph of his scrotum,
the size of the biggest collective farm pumpkin, is
also reprinted in foreign medical books, wherever
elephantiasis (elephantiasis nostras) is mentioned,
and as a moral for writers that to write one must have
more than big balls.*

Broken up into seven short tales, Danilo Kiš's *A Tomb for Boris
Davidovich* chronicles the lives of revolutionaries and how the
revolutions they support eventually destroy them. Each of
the seven short tales stands alone as a miniature biography of
one of the revolutionaries, with minor references to previous
characters scattered throughout. From a Jewish tailor whose
revolutionary fervor drives him to horrible crimes, to a
murder based on a Tarot reading, the characters within Kiš's
novel each represent the weight of rebellion and the cruelty
of the established system. In the final story, Darmolatov, a
revolutionary poet, suffers from an acute case of elephantiasis,
causing his testicles to swell to the size of a pumpkin. Kiš, in
the last line of the novel, hilariously pays homage to the bravery

of men and women who stand up in the face of oppression, no matter the cost.

TAKE IT OR LEAVE IT
Raymond Federman
-
1976

[So long everybody!]

Raymond Federman's *Take It or Leave It* passes through multiple narrative filters before reaching its reader. Focused around the story of an individual known only as "the old man," the narration comes courtesy of Moinous and Manredef, friends of the old man who were told the tale by the man himself. They are, in turn, telling the story to an in-text representation of Federman and, by proxy, the reader. In a muddled attempt at preserving the old man's history, and as a result immortalizing him, the narrators include the old man's past and present almost simultaneously. The novel struggles with the idea of summarizing a lifetime to an outsider, and how people's perceptions of others shape history. The last line mirrors the closing lines of a performance. The reader has learned about the life of the old man, and in turn, is expected to carry it with them, thereby continuing the story with their own unreliability.

SONG OF SOLOMON

Toni Morrison

-

1977

For now he knew what Shalimar knew: If you surrendered to the air, you could ride it.

Toni Morrison's novel *Song of Solomon* centers around African American identity and the discovery of self. The protagonist, Milkman, a morally fickle character who struggles to find purpose in his life, tries to track down a golden treasure rumored to have been hidden by his grandfather. Following the advice of his aunt Pilate, an intensely spiritual woman who holds tightly to her past, Milkman travels into the backcountry of the South to seek out his fortune. Loosely following the southward path of his distant ancestor Shalimar, an escaped slave renamed Solomon by the slave traders who brought him to America, Milkman finally finds a sense of belonging. Hunted down by Guitar, a childhood friend and member of the Seven Days society, a terrorist organization that kills white women and children, Milkman lets go of his fear and faces his death head-on. Like Shalimar, he has found his place outside of the confines of oppression, and with that he is finally able to fly.

THE PUBLIC BURNING
Robert Coover
-
1977

"Vaya con Dios, my darklin, and remember: vote early and vote often, don't take any wooden nickels, and"—by now I was rolling about helplessly on the spare-room floor, scrunched up around my throbbing pain and bawling like a baby—"always leave 'em laughin' as you say good-bye!"

Robert Coover said that he wanted *The Public Burning* "to seem to have been written by the whole nation through all of its history." No doubt this is why the book has been consistently relevant since its publication. Narrated by the character of Richard Nixon, the novel focuses on the events leading up to the public execution of Julius and Ethel Rosenberg, and features a cast of famous political figures, including a larger-than-life Uncle Sam who spouts pop culture references and profanity alike. Nixon is tasked with proving the Rosenbergs' guilt and becomes consumed by his obsession with Ethel. In the last scene, the Rosenbergs are electrocuted publicly. Nixon, in a graphic metaphor for his ideological destruction at the hands of the American system, is raped by Uncle Sam. In the last lines, Nixon lies prone on the floor of the execution chamber, listening to a string of useless advice from Uncle Sam that lingers long after he leaves him behind.

ARTHUR REX
Thomas Berger
-
1978

But in these fair laps we must leave King Arthur, who was never historical, but everything he did was true.

Thomas Berger's *Arthur Rex* is a retelling of the classic tale of King Arthur. With a narrator reminiscent of the classic medieval epic, Berger's oftentimes humorous story takes the once-shallow characters and provides new depth that exposes a number of problematic truths inherent to the story. From the sexually inept Percival to the cynical Guinevere, the stoic heroes of legend become a group of flawed and deeply sad humans who hide behind religious ideology and willful ignorance. This new bent on the heroic tale is not meant to cast doubt on the legends, but rather to redefine heroism and instill hope into the reader. The once-righteous and unrelatable King Arthur suddenly becomes a man of modern times—one who struggles with feelings of uncertainty and loneliness like anyone. He doesn't have to defeat knights and pull swords from stones to overcome these struggles, he simply has to acknowledge them. Through this vulnerability, the character of King Arthur, though the stuff of legend, becomes just as real as any of those whom history has forgotten.

THE BOOK OF LAUGHTER AND FORGETTING
Milan Kundera
-
1979

The others listened with interest, their naked genitals staring dully, sadly, listlessly at the yellow sand.

Milan Kundera's *The Book of Laughter and Forgetting* was the first novel that he wrote following his exile from Czechoslovakia to France, which clearly affected the tone of the text. *The Book of Laughter and Forgetting* consists of seven independent narratives, all of which deal with memory in some way. The final story of the collection, called "The Border," ties the bliss of forgetting to the fleeting nature of pleasure as the central character of the story, Jan, prepares to cross a physical border into the unknown. After an absurd farewell orgy, Jan meets with nudists on a beach, who discuss political and social theories. The final lines show the characters prioritizing societal awareness over physical pleasure, stepping away from the motif of forgetfulness and instead moving toward enlightenment and true change.

MULLIGAN STEW
Gilbert Sorrentino
-
1979

". . . and to all you other cats and chicks out there, sweet or otherwise, buried deep in wordy tombs, who never yet have walked from off the page, a shake and a hug and a kiss and a drink. Cheers!"

After more than 20 rejections from publishers, *Mulligan Stew* finally found a home at Grove Press in 1978. Most likely, the industry reluctance was because the book was, quite accurately, a literary stew. It details the struggles of Anthony Lamont, a writer whose work, be it rambling journal entries or erotic poems, comprises the majority of the text. The story is told through multiple layers, including glimpses into the life of Anthony and the frustrations of the main characters, who are most notably lifted from other works of fiction. With a cast list that includes Ned Beaumont from *The Glass Key* by Dashiell Hammett and Martin Halpin from *Finnegans Wake* by James Joyce, the story rapidly spirals out of Anthony's control, and Halpin fears that the author has died. Halpin ends on a well-wishing note for all the characters who may never get their chance in the sun, a nod to the difficulties *Mulligan Stew* had getting published.

IF ON A WINTER'S NIGHT A TRAVELER
Italo Calvino
-
1979

"And you say, 'Just a moment, I've almost finished

If on a winter's night a

traveler

by Italo Calvino.'"

Italo Calvino's postmodern book *If on a winter's night a traveler* is broken down into 22 separate sections, each following a different narrative structure and storyline. Shifting between third-, second-, and first-person narrative viewpoints, the reader is addressed as the main character of the story, a main character whose goal is to finish reading Italo Calvino's *If on a winter's night a traveler*. Eventually, the main character/reader meets Ludmilla, who is also trying to read *If on a winter's night a traveler*. The main character/reader ends up marrying

Ludmilla (congratulations!) and they both try and finish reading Calvino's novel. The story ends in the same way that it began, restarting the cyclical story that pushes the limits of what a novel can be.

HOW GERMAN IS IT
Walter Abish
-
1980

Is it possible for anyone in Germany, nowadays, to raise his right hand, for whatever the reason, and not be flooded by the memory of a dream to end all dreams?

In his most celebrated novel, *How German Is It*, Walter Abish probes a nation in transition, exploring what it means to be a citizen of Germany following the horrific events of the Holocaust. The central characters in his story, two brothers whose father opposed Hitler's regime at the cost of his own life, must attempt to rebuild their identities separate from their nationality, a task only possible through educating themselves about the past. Throughout the novel, both brothers find themselves the targets of violent threats, and struggle with the knowledge that their town is the site of one of the many Holocaust death camps, a fact that the local government tries to cover up. In the last line, Abish seems to question if Germany will ever recover from its past actions, a haunting sentiment that lingers with the reader long after the book is closed.

WILD SEED
Octavia E. Butler
-
1980

He laughed. He did not care what she called herself as long as she went on living. And she would do that. No matter where she went, she would live. She would not leave him.

Set prior to the events of the other novels in her Patternist series, Octavia Butler's *Wild Seed* is the story of two immortal African mutants. The protagonist, a woman named Anyanwu, possesses the ability to heal herself and others and to shape-shift into animals. The antagonist, a man named Doro, is a spirit who moves into a human host and drains their life force. Obsessed with the idea of breeding superhumans, Doro convinces Anyanwu to marry his son, Isaac, another mutant. Doro feels threatened by Anyanwu's powers and wishes her dead, but allows her to live due to her successful marriage to Isaac. Eventually, Isaac dies and Anyanwu flees Doro's clutches. After years of searching, Doro finally finds Anyanwu in Louisiana, building a community for other superhumans. When Doro takes over the community, Anyanwu decides to kill herself instead of suffering in Doro's clutches. Terrified at the prospect of being alone, Doro repents of his actions and they agree to work together to help their people prosper. In the final lines, Anyanwu takes on the name Emma, meaning *ancestor* or *grandmother*, solidifying her commitment to helping her people thrive.

HOUSEKEEPING
Marilynne Robinson
-
1980

No one watching this woman smear her initials in the steam on her water glass with her first finger, or slip cellophane packets of oyster crackers into her handbag for the sea gulls, could know how her thoughts are thronged by our absence, or know how she does not watch, does not listen, does not wait, does not hope, and always for me and Sylvie.

Marilynne Robinson's debut novel, *Housekeeping,* is about two orphaned sisters, Ruth and Lucille Stone, whose lives are altered by their aunt Sylvie. Sylvie is an eccentric woman, a drifter who seems always on the brink of leaving the two girls to once again care for themselves or live with some other willing guardian. Ruth admires the restless spirit of her aunt, while Lucille wants nothing more than stability, and pushes against Sylvie's spell. The divergence in attitude only grows, and as it does we come face-to-face with two opposing ways of life: restlessness or stability. In the end, it is Sylvie and Ruth who break through the human condition by burning down their home and riding the rails, while Lucille lives a respectably quaint life in Boston, never longing for what could have been, but always thinking about Sylvie and Ruth.

DISTANT RELATIONS
Carlos Fuentes
-
1980

No one remembers the whole story.

The plot of Carlos Fuentes's *Distant Relations* is, at times, complex and hard to follow. The novel opens in the elegant dining room of the Automobile Club de France, where Branly, the narrator and protagonist, tells a story to a fictionalized Carlos Fuentes. Branly reminisces about his encounter with Hugo Heredia, a Mexican archaeologist, and his son, Victor. Victor and Branly play a lighthearted game in which they look through the phonebook for anyone who shares Victor's name and decide to seek out the other Victor Heredia. Through a complicated series of distant connections, Branly and Victor become trapped by the other Victor Heredia thanks to a childhood argument. The plot devolves from there, straddling the line between realism and fantasy. In the end, the reader gets the impression that not even Branly knows the story, and that it is reformed with every telling.

WAITING FOR THE BARBARIANS

J. M. Coetzee

-

1980

This is not the scene I dreamed of. Like much else nowadays I leave it feeling stupid, like a man who lost his way long ago but presses on along a road that may lead nowhere.

J. M. Coetzee's novel *Waiting for the Barbarians* ends on a note of cleansing hope in an otherwise bleak tale of colonization and imperial violence. Following an unnamed magistrate of a small town in "the Empire," Coetzee's novel centers around issues of racism, prejudice, and what it means to be "civilized." When the magistrate's town is occupied by Empire soldiers who are supposedly preparing for an imminent barbarian attack, the magistrate witnesses the torture and murder of a family of barbarians firsthand. When a blind barbarian beggar makes her way into the town, the magistrate begins to rethink his stance on barbarians and helps the girl return to her people. On his way back to the village, the magistrate is thrown in prison by the soldiers for assisting the girl, but ultimately regains his freedom. With the preemptive war against the barbarians lost and the town ransacked by the retreating soldiers, the magistrate realizes his people are no different than the barbarian tribes camped in the distance. In the final lines, the barbarians have still not attacked the town, and we are left with the possibility of positive transformation as the magistrate realizes that his future is nothing like he dreamed it would be.

A CONFEDERACY OF DUNCES
John Kennedy Toole

-

1980

Taking the pigtail in one of his paws, he pressed it warmly to his wet moustache.

Published posthumously, John Kennedy Toole's *A Confederacy of Dunces* follows the life and antics of Ignatius Reilly, an overweight, mustachioed layabout who spends most of his days praising medieval philosophy and faulting society for its perversion. Pressed by his mother to get a job, Ignatius is hired by the Levy Pants company. Instead of working, Ignatius pens a false letter to a retailer using his boss's name and leads an unsuccessful workers' revolution at the factory to impress his long-distance girlfriend, Myrna Minkoff. Ignatius is fired and gets a second job running a hot dog stand. Meanwhile, Jones, the floor sweeper at a local strip club, starts an elaborate setup to get his boss in trouble that leads to Ignatius unknowingly storing pornographic materials in his cart. Through a complicated turn of events, Ignatius's mother decides to send him to a mental asylum, but Ignatius evades institutionalization thanks to Myrna. In the last lines, we see a tender gesture at the hands of a repulsive but entertaining individual as he finally makes his way out into the world at large.

THE NAME OF THE ROSE

Umberto Eco

-

1980

"*I leave this manuscript, I do not know for whom, I no longer know what it is about:* stat rosa pristina nomine, nomina nuda tenemus."

Umberto Eco's *The Name of the Rose* is a murder mystery set in early 14th-century Italy. The story takes place at the Aedificium, a large monastery with a library of historic and sacred texts of immense importance. As inhabitants of the monastery continue to die in mysterious ways, it becomes clear that the deaths connect to a specific book in the library: the second volume of Aristotle's *Poetics*. The culprit is an old monk named Jorge, who poisoned the pages, causing anyone who reads it to perish. His motive, it seems, stemmed from his hatred of laughter. In the end, Jorge destroys the book and burns down the library, thus erasing them from existence. The story ends with Adso, a surviving monk, finishing the text that we have been reading. He leaves us with one final thought: "the ancient rose remains by its name; naked names are all that we have." That which has perished, he thinks, remains with us in name and name alone.

THE TRANSIT OF VENUS
Shirley Hazzard
-
1980

Within the cabin, nothing could be heard. Only, as the plane rose from the ground, a long hiss of air— like the intake of humanity's breath when a work of ages shrivels in an instant; or the great gasp of hull and ocean as a ship goes down.

Shirley Hazzard's novel *The Transit of Venus* is reminiscent of a 19th-century romance novel. It tells the story of two sisters, Caroline and Grace Bell, both of whom move from Australia to England in the 1950s. Unlike many 19th-century romances, however, Hazzard's characters seem doomed to tragedy from the start. Though not explicitly stated in the closing lines, their fate is clear to the attentive reader. As Caroline sits on a plane bound for Rome, she notices a doctor who had treated her not long ago. The realization of Caroline's impending demise will only reach dedicated readers, as the doctor was introduced 50 pages earlier with the offhand detail that he would die in a plane crash on his way to Rome three months later. It is not just Caroline's imminent death that closes the book with a shudder, it is the implication that, much like the transit of Venus, chance meetings can impact our lives more drastically than we realize.

MIDNIGHT'S CHILDREN

Salman Rushdie

-

1981

*... It is the privilege and the curse of midnight's
children to be both masters and victims of their times,
to forsake privacy and be sucked into the annihilating
whirlpool of the multitudes, and to be unable to live
or die in peace.*

Salman Rushdie's work *Midnight's Children* follows the story
of Saleem Sinai, a boy born at exactly midnight on August 15,
1947, the day of India's independence from British rule. Saleem
possesses telepathic powers, which he uses to contact the other
children born on the night of August 15. Saleem learns that each
of the Midnight Children possess unique powers depending
on how close to midnight they were born. Threatened by
the powers of the Midnight Children, Indira Gandhi, the
prime minister of India, starts a forced sterilization campaign,
destroying the Midnight Children's futures one by one. On the
cusp of his 31st birthday, Saleem shares his life story with his
lover and companion, Padma, prophesizing the fate of future
Midnight Children, who are always balanced on the edge of
history, their lives linked to the fate of their nation, even in
their death. Saleem's final words accept his insignificance in the
face of the oncoming generations, where each Midnight Child

will give up their own freedom to help their nation live in a never-ending cycle.

OH WHAT A PARADISE IT SEEMS
John Cheever
-
1982

But that is another tale, and as I said in the beginning, this is just a story meant to be read in bed in an old house on a rainy night.

Oh What a Paradise It Seems was the last work of fiction published by John Cheever prior to his death in 1982, and many consider the novella to be his best work. The short novel tells the story of Lemuel Sears, an aging executive chasing love, lust, and youth. In typical Cheever fashion, elements of suburban life are interwoven with horrors which, though seemingly out of place, go hand in hand with the banal. The central conflict of the story involves a village pond that Sears ice-skates on every winter. Sears loves twirling about on the pure, frozen water, but as the pond becomes increasingly more polluted, so too does Sears, who desperately tries to hold on to his youth through a series of affairs. In the end, the paradise that once brought so much joy to the aging man may have been temporarily rescued, but it cannot be forever preserved. Cheever seems to try and alleviate the weight of the story in his final lines, brushing aside Sears's desperation as a horror story meant for late-night reading and nothing more.

THE COLOR PURPLE
Alice Walker
-
1982

But I don't think us feel old at all. And us so happy.
Matter of fact, I think this the youngest us ever felt.

Alice Walker made history with her novel *The Color Purple* when she won the Pulitzer Prize for Fiction in 1983, making her the first black woman to receive this honor. The acclaimed novel details the experience of African American women in the 1930s American South. Celie, the protagonist, is a woman who has been abused all her life. From her father to the man she is forced to marry, the male presence in the book is overwhelmingly negative. Celie forms an inseparable bond with a group of abused and independent women throughout the book, the most significant of whom is her sister, Nettie, who escaped their abusive father to live in Africa with her children. Before long, Celie gains the courage to leave her abusive husband, Albert, and begins pursuing a life of independence.

After many decades apart, Nettie returns to America with her husband, Reverend Samuel, and the sisters reunite. Finally free to live their lives the way they want to, both women feel that, even in their old age, they have never felt so young.

WATCHING FATHER DIE
B. H. Friedman
-
1982

I am looking now into a mirror, watching Father die. Behind me my son and daughter stand, also watching Father die.

B. H. Friedman's *Coming Close* is a collection of four stories that deal with the events that make up a man's life. "Watching Father Die" is the longest piece in the collection. It details the experience of a man coming to terms with the death of his father, both in a physical and metaphorical sense. Told through a series of memories, the father's dialog is presented in capital letters to show the weight they carried in the son's mind. Slowly, the godlike image of the father starts to fade, and the son is forced to realize that his father is mortal, subject to flaws, illnesses, and death like any other man. In the last lines, the son finds himself standing in front of the mirror as his children realize that their father is not the mythic being they thought, continuing the cycle for another generation.

THE NAMES
Don DeLillo
-
1982

It was the nightmare of real things, the fallen wonder of the world.

While a book that sets out to examine the complexities of language runs the risk of spiraling into a scarcely comprehensible study of semiotics, Don DeLillo's *The Names* is at once an international thriller and a philosophical exploration of spoken communication. At the center of the story is James Axton, an American working in Athens as a risk analyst. An unwitting CIA agent, Axton finds himself tracking a murderous cult across multiple countries. The motif throughout is the danger of language as a method of control, whether it be in religion, politics, or even the sexual interactions between two individuals. The abuse and manipulation of language eventually results in the characters' inability to find meaning, which in turn leaves the reader struggling to find meaning. By the end, language crumbles, and, presumably, society is not far behind.

THE DEATH OF CHE GUEVARA
Jay Cantor
-
1983

*Begin again! It all must be done over! 1976 1977
1978 1979 1980 1981 1982 1983 1984*

In Jay Cantor's debut novel, *The Death of Che Guevara*, the fictionalized history of the Marxist guerrilla leader Che Guevara is explored and exploited. Facts are cherry-picked based on their function within the story, and the result is a captivating story that, when viewed in the right light, appears as biography, a fiction piece, or even a philosophical study of what is truth. At times, actual historical accounts of Che's relationship with Fidel Castro, his involvement in the Cuban Revolution, and his warfare tactics are detailed in high accuracy; at other times, stories are composed based on contextual information, with Che admitting to fabricating the death of his father for anecdotal purposes. The story is rewritten time and time again, much like the revolution. In the last pages, Ponco, the character responsible for piecing together Che's final days, seemingly decries the ideology of the author himself and demands that he try again. "Do better this time," he seems to say. "¡Viva la Revolución!"

ANGELS

Denis Johnson

-

1983

But that was just a story, something that people will tell themselves, something to pass the time it takes for the violence inside a man to wear him away, or to be consumed itself, depending on who is the candle and who is the light.

Described as "a mixture of poetry and obscenity," by *New York Times* critic Alice Hoffman, Denis Johnson's first novel, *Angels*, took 12 years to write. In the novel, Jamie and her two children meet Bill Houston on a bus to Hershey, Pennsylvania—a man whose drunken, broken bitterness was birthed in Vietnam. Jamie, who left Oakland, California, to escape her husk of a husband, takes up with Bill and the two descend into madness together. Jamie becomes addicted to pills and is checked into a mental institution; Bill robs a bank and ends up murdering one of the guards. Only Jamie has the purpose or luck to climb back out into the world, while Bill meets his end in a gas chamber. The story closes on Fredericks, a criminal lawyer, contemplating the execution of Bill, a man who, for all his misdeeds, Fredericks wanted to help. The light only shines through these characters in a few moments throughout this novel as they consume themselves in search of something brighter.

THE ASSASSINATION OF JESSE JAMES BY THE COWARD ROBERT FORD

Ron Hansen

-

1983

His body jolted backward, jolted the floorboards, and Ella Mae Waterson screamed, but Robert Ford only looked at the ceiling, the light going out of his eyes before he could say the right words.

The life of famous American outlaw Jesse James is the subject of Ron Hansen's historical *The Assassination of Jesse James by the Coward Robert Ford*, though Jesse is not the main character. Robert "Bob" Ford is the novel's protagonist, the brother of one of Jesse's men. While he was accepted into Jesse James's outer circle, Bob finds himself enticed by the prize on Jesse's head. After a convoluted turn of events in which Bob frames one of Jesse's men, Jesse includes Bob in the planning of a bank robbery. Bob seizes his chance and kills the unarmed Jesse, securing the paltry reward and leaving himself and his bother destitute and in search of work. While the death of Jesse James is at the climax of the novel, the final lines center around Bob. Bob, now the owner of a successful business in Colorado, is killed in cold blood by Soapy Smith, a man seeking the same kind of glory that drove Bob to kill Jesse. Killed without warning, neither Bob nor Jesse can speak to their own actions; the story of their death lives on as a memorial to the Wild West.

THE UNBEARABLE LIGHTNESS OF BEING
Milan Kundera
-
1984

Up out of the lampshade, startled by the overhead light, flew a large nocturnal butterfly that began circling the room. The strains of the piano and violin rose up weakly from below.

Friedrich Nietzsche wrote extensively about the nature of time, specifically the concept of "eternal recurrence," which suggests that a finite number of events will repeat an infinite number of times, and we are merely caught in the loop. *The Unbearable Lightness of Being* by Milan Kundera operates under the much more romantic belief that all of us have but one life to live, so we should make it count. Centered around Tomáš, his wife, Tereza, and his lover, Sabina, the novel explores the duality of lightness and heaviness and the effects of Russia's invasion of Czechoslovakia. Through a tangled web of interpersonal relationships, Tomáš and Tereza decide to escape to Switzerland, where they document the events of the invasion. Once they realize the outside world does not care about the events of their homeland, they return to Czechoslovakia, knowing they will not be able to leave again. In the final line, the unbearable temporality of human life is held up against the life of a butterfly and a musical note, two other things whose immense beauty is paired with a tragically ephemeral existence.

WHITE NOISE
Don DeLillo
-
1985

Everything we need that is not food or love is here in the tabloid racks. The tales of the supernatural and extraterrestrial. The miracle vitamins, the cures for cancer, the remedies for obesity. The cults of the famous and the dead.

Much of Don DeLillo's work focuses on a specific aspect of society and masterfully examines it. In *White Noise*, his focus is consumerism. The main character of the novel, Jack Gladney, is a professor at a small Midwestern college. He and his wife, Babette, are terrified of death and spend much of the novel trying to find ways to alleviate their fear. After a chemical accident forces them to briefly evacuate their hometown, Jack discovers Babette's addiction to Dylar, an experimental drug produced to eliminate the fear of death. During a discussion with a colleague, Jack decides that the best way to rid himself of his own fear is by killing someone else. After wounding his wife's lover, Willie Mink, Jack realizes his foolishness and brings Willie to the hospital, deciding to instead focus his attention on the living. In the final lines, DeLillo hones in on the American Dream, where human needs are reduced to tabloids, dead celebrities, and chemicals.

PERFUME: THE STORY OF A MURDERER

Patrick Süskind

-

1985

When they finally did dare it, at first with stolen glances then candid ones, they had to smile. They were uncommonly proud. For the first time they had done something out of Love.

Grenouille, the protagonist of Patrick Süskind's novel *Perfume: The Story of a Murderer*, has a remarkable sense of smell, which compels him to kill young women. To Grenouille, scent is the only way people can love each other, and so he considers his murders, which he commits to preserve the women's scent by means of perfume, an act of love. In the end, he succeeds in bottling the ultimate scent. Though he is caught for the murder and sentenced to death thanks to the considerable evidence against him, Grenouille applies some of his perfect perfume and wins over the crowd as he walks to his execution. So convincing is the innocence he is exuding that even the father of the girl he murdered offers to adopt him. But this does nothing to help the misanthropic Grenouille, who pours an entire bottle of this innocent essence over himself and gets himself torn apart by a raving crowd in the streets of Paris.

IN COUNTRY
Bobbie Ann Mason

-

1985

He is sitting there cross-legged in front of the wall, and slowly his face bursts into a smile like flames.

Bobbie Ann Mason's first novel, *In Country*, chronicles the private fallout experienced not only by veterans of the war in Vietnam, but by those whom they returned home to. Sam Hughes is the novel's protagonist, a high school girl whose father died in Vietnam. She lives in rural Kentucky with her uncle Emmett, who suffers from the aftereffects of Agent Orange exposure and tries to find ways to process his own mental trauma. The novel focuses on Sam's attempt to cope with something she knows little about. It is only through reading her father's diary and learning about the horrors of the war that Sam begins to come to terms with her world. Her father transitions from someone larger than life to an ordinary person caught up in a horrible conflict. In the final lines, Sam and Emmett visit the Vietnam War Memorial. In his first true moment of acknowledgment, Emmett reads the names on the monument and smiles as the tremendous burden of the war finally lifts off of his shoulders.

CONTINENTAL DRIFT
Russell Banks
-
1985

Go, my book, and help destroy the world as it is.

Russell Banks's ambitious novel *Continental Drift* turns the idea of the American Dream on its head. Bob, an average blue-collar man living in New Hampshire and struggling against debt, dreams of moving to Florida and striking it rich like his brother. Vanise Dorsinville is a Haitian immigrant who decides to leave her life in Haiti with her nephew and infant son for the coast of Florida. Both individuals are so dissatisfied with their lives that the balmy air of Florida seems enough to save them. In the opening lines of the novel, we know these characters' lives are to end in tragedy. Bob moves to Florida with his wife and children only to find himself surrounded by crime and violence; Vanise barely survives being thrown overboard from the ship smuggling her to America. At the close of the novel, Banks seems to call for the book to change society for the better—to reduce violence and make the American Dream what it once was. A tall order for both reader and book alike.

ALWAYS COMING HOME
Ursula K. Le Guin
-
1985

And behold the Geomancer, whose name measures the Valley, who shaped the hills and helped me sink half California, who went on the Salt Journey, caught the Train, and walked every step with Grey Bull—Heya Heggaia, han es im! Amoud gewakwasur, yeshou gewakwasur.

Detailing a postapocalyptic California, Ursula K. Le Guin's *Always Coming Home* presents a world which retains some qualities of our own while remaining entirely unique. Centered around two opposing tribes, the Kesh and the Condor, Le Guin's novel pits the peaceful, matrilineal society of the Kesh against the violent patriarchy of the Condor. In a book told part through story, part through song, and part through anthropological narrative, Le Guin explores the ravages of an overly violent society. Rich with histories, languages, and cultures unique to the world of sunken California, this novel explores Western society through the lens of anthropology, allowing what is familiar to become new and malleable. The final lines, which echo the tone of an epic poem, are entirely comprehensible to the dedicated reader, bringing Le Guin's world to life on and off the page.

BLOOD MERIDIAN
Cormac McCarthy
-
1985

His feet are light and nimble. He never sleeps. He says that he will never die. He dances in light and in shadow and he is a great favorite. He never sleeps, the judge. He is dancing, dancing. He says that he will never die.

With the protagonist, known only as "the kid," presumably killed by Judge Holden, all the reader is left with at the end of Cormac McCarthy's classic novel is the image of this enigmatic character skillfully and wildly dancing in the nude. The novel itself centers around the kid, a runaway who was born during a meteor storm and turned to a life of almost unimaginable violence. After joining Joel Glanton's gang, the kid runs into Judge Holden. After hundreds of pages and dozens of horrific deeds, the judge has left nothing but destruction in his wake, and by the end we still do not understand his motive, or if he is even human. In the judge, McCarthy created an embodiment of pure evil, a thing of immense power that wants only to cause pain and to revel in it. With the kid, our last bastion against the judge, out of the picture, the celebration commences. And when the personification of evil says he will never die, we believe him.

THE HANDMAID'S TALE

Margaret Atwood

-

1985

"Are there any questions?"

The Handmaid's Tale, Margaret Atwood's dystopian novel set in a future America ruled by a totalitarian Christian government, is one of the rare novels that earned a spot in college classrooms almost as soon as it hit shelves. The story stands as a pillar of contemporary feminist literature. Offred, the novel's protagonist, lives in the religious totalitarian government of Gilead as an enslaved handmaid for the Commander. Stripped of her rights and treated like property, Offred's sole purpose is to bear children for the Commander in place of his infertile wife. Offred is eventually able to escape Gilead through the help of the Mayday resistance and passes down her story through a set of cassette tapes. In the last portion of the novel, we see professors analyzing Offred's story, emphasizing that there is no way to prove her story to be true, as all records have been destroyed aside from her cassettes. In the final lines, the story itself seems to be daring us to question its legitimacy and remain suspicious of the powerful in our present society.

RAT MAN OF PARIS
Paul West
-
1986

All his dithers, his fumbles, his loving, wished away by a bold, heroic thumbprint from his last adieu, which he makes with his fist held aloft, the thumb upright.

Etienne Poulsifer, also known as the Rat Man of Paris, is the enigmatic, feral subject of Paul West's novel of the same name. Based on the real-life Rat Man who used to shove dirty rodents in the faces of passersby in the streets of Paris, West gives motive and humanity to this strange figure. He is a man who acts to forget the deaths of his fellow villagers at the hands of the Nazis, an event which traumatized him into the twisted, obsessive husk who occupies a darkened room in Paris. Though he does not know what it will accomplish, he continues on with these bizarre artistic expressions, lost in a clouded haze. Eventually, Rat Man finds Sharli, a schoolteacher who tries to care for him and who eventually has a child with him. In the end, we cannot be sure that things will change permanently for Rat Man. He continues in an odd haze filled with loving, forgetting, and wandering, giving the reader a thumbs-up in the concluding sentence as if to let them know they can leave his story now, even though he cannot see which way his life is going anymore.

THE SPORTSWRITER
Richard Ford
-
1986

And in truth, of course, this may be the last time that you will ever feel this way again.

Richard Ford's *The Sportswriter* is the first novel in a series that he has described as "The Bascombe Novels." Frank Bascombe, the protagonist of the series, is a novelist turned sportswriter who glides through life relatively undisturbed and entirely lethargic until the death of his son. The narrative picks up several years after this passing, and Frank's life has since gone to shambles. His erratic behavior causes his marriage to fall apart, and he struggles to understand how his now ex-wife can lead a seemingly happy life following such an immense tragedy. All of his attempts at normalcy seem to only make him more miserable as he continues to fail in his relationships and stumble through life without purpose. It is only through a trip to Florida to fulfill his dead friend's wishes that Frank seems to find some peace. As he walks shirtless along the beach in the final pages of the novel, the burden of his son's death briefly lifts. His period of mourning, he thinks, is over. Frank basks in this feeling, appreciating the world around him, because he knows he may never feel this way again.

ROGER'S VERSION
John Updike
-
1986

"Where on earth are you going?" I asked her.

"Obviously," she said, "to church."

"Why would you do a ridiculous thing like that?"

"Oh—" She appraised me with her pale green eyes. Whatever emotions had washed through her had left an amused glint, a hint or seed. In her gorgeous rounded woman's voice she pronounced smilingly, "To annoy you."

Rarely do science and the notion of a traditional God go hand in hand, but in John Updike's novel *Roger's Version*, the two are married together out of monomaniacal desire to prove the existence of the latter. The themes of spirituality and practicality are both at odds and coexistent in this novel, a trait found in many of Updike's works. Roger, a professor of divinity, takes an interest in a graduate student named Dale, who sets out to prove God's existence with computer science, a desire which both frustrates and intrigues Roger. The two become tied up not only in divinity but also through sex, as Dale begins to sleep with Roger's wife, Esther, while Roger begins an affair with his own niece, Verna. In the end, God does not exist, at least according to Dale's computer program. However, it seems Roger and Esther's marriage has gotten a second wind, as the playful banter the novel closes on is that of newlyweds.

CHRISTOPHER UNBORN

Carlos Fuentes

-

1987

... He is the Baroque Angel, with a sword in his hand and quetzal wings, and a serpent doublet, and a golden helmet, the Angel strikes, strikes the lips of the boy being born on the beach: the burning and painful sword strikes his lips and the boy forgets, he forgets everything forgets everything, f

o

r

g

e

t

s

Carlos Fuentes's novel *Christopher Unborn* is set in 1992 Mexico. The story provides a grim outlook of the future, with major economic disparity affecting the majority of Mexicans. Though the subject is bleak, the tone is anything but. Fuentes consistently injects humor into the plot, which is narrated by an intellectually gifted fetus named Christopher, whose birth is scheduled to arrive 500 years after Columbus landed in America. Following a nine-chapter structure that represents Christopher's life from conception to birth, the story follows Angel, Christopher's father, as he strives to stay honest in Mexico's corrupt political climate. In the final lines, Christopher gets one final glimpse of heavenly glory before being born, an event that will force him to forget everything that has passed through his brilliant mind.

THE BROOM OF THE SYSTEM
David Foster Wallace
-
1987

"You can trust me," R.V. said, watching her hand. "I'm a man of my"

David Foster Wallace began writing his first novel, *The Broom of the System,* when he was an undergraduate at Amherst College. The book largely examines the relationship between language and identity. A prime example of metafiction, *The Broom of the System* operates as both fiction and scientific amalgamation, switching back and forth between the two until the main character's reality has gone from strange to entirely improbable. The final line cleverly plays with the notion of language and our relationship to it. Wallace cuts Rick Vigorous off mid-sentence, but only omits one word. Based on contextual clues, we could assume that Rick meant to say "I'm a man of my word." But if the reader has learned anything from Wallace, they know they cannot make that assumption. Simply because we have heard that arrangement of words countless times before does not mean that is what we are about to hear, or that we will ever hear it again.

SUCH WAS THE SEASON
Clarence Major
-
1987

I just have to believe that this one ain't much worse than the baddest we ever faced.

Clarence Major's *Such Was the Season* ends with a weariness felt by someone who has had to work hard their entire life to survive. The story's narrator is Annie Eliza Hicks, an elderly black woman whose wisdom is subtle but absolute. At the center of the story's conflict is Annie's son Jeremiah, a wealthy gospel preacher whose wife, Renee, has a promising career in politics. Renee wishes to use her platform in order to expose corruption in the produce industry, but little does she know that one of the primary sources of said corruption is none other than

Jeremiah. The conflict unfolds from the perspective of Annie, who closes the story with a sentiment that is somehow somber and uplifting: they have seen some awful years; whatever may come will be faced with strength.

THE MESSIAH OF STOCKHOLM
Cynthia Ozick
-
1987

And then, in the blue light of Stockholm among zebra fumes, he grieved.

Bruno Schulz is often regarded as one of the great writers of the 20th century. Tragically, he lost his life during the Nazi occupation of Drohobycz in 1942 and much of his work was lost during the Holocaust, including the unfinished manuscript of his book *The Messiah*. This missing text is what Cynthia Ozick's novella *The Messiah of Stockholm* revolves around. The protagonist, Lars Andemening, is a literary critic of unsubstantial recognition who sustains himself on the unconfirmed knowledge that he is the son of Bruno Schulz. When contacted by Adela, a woman who claims to be Schulz's illegitimate daughter and who may be in possession of the fabled *Messiah* manuscript, Lars's identity is challenged. He feels unable to share in the glory of having an ancestor such as

Schulz, and in the final pages of the story burns the manuscript for *The Messiah*. Now, as Lars contemplates the "zebra fumes" of all the burned, uniform-clad bodies of the millions of Jews killed in the Holocaust, he ceases to think of himself, and he grieves not only for Schulz, but for every Jewish man, woman, and child consumed by those terrible flames.

YOU BRIGHT AND RISEN ANGELS
William T. Vollmann
-
1987

But I knew that Catherine had kissed me because she trusted me, and that made me happy then but now I am sad because by the time my eyes close each night I suspect that as usual I have been fooling myself, that she, too, is in her grave.

The final sentence of William Vollmann's debut novel, *You Bright and Risen Angels,* is, in a way, deceptive. The nearly 700-page book detailing the uprising of a group of humanoid insects against the human world plays out like an experiment in fiction. The novel uses a postmodern approach to explore the role of electricity in modern society. These unique and, at times, inaccessible methods of storytelling culminate in an ending that, though disappointing to some, reads like a contemporary story. In the last lines, there is an air of normalcy as the speaker falls asleep, wondering about his lost Catherine and questioning, it seems, if the revolution was worth the cost after all.

THE CARPATHIANS
Janet Frame
-
1988

What exists, though, is the memory of events known and imagined, and the use of words to continue the memory through centuries, despite or with the Gravity Star, to a future when today, our Now, will be known as our past has been known as Ancient Springtime, while we, who treasure the Memory Flower, are the housekeepers of Ancient Springtime.

The Carpathians, the last novel Janet Frame released before her death, follows a wealthy, wanderlust-driven New York native named Mattina Brecon as she travels to a fictional New Zealand town called Puamahara to alleviate her boredom. Once in Puamahara, Brecon seeks two mystical objects: the Memory Flower, which links the memories of a place with its inhabitants to create a never-ending history, and the Gravity Star, which appears both close and infinitely far away at the same time. The novel, like the phenomena themselves, is a thing which eludes comprehension. Its narrative structure seems to almost unravel by design as the Memory Flower and Gravity Star distort the fabric of reality. In the end, Brecon is taken by illness. As she lies dying, she begs her husband to go to Puamahara and document the mysterious occurrences in writing. Ultimately, it is Mattina's son and our narrator, John, who fulfills her wishes. The last line mirrors the flexibility of time and reality in the story, and reminds us that everyone, no matter how young or old, is responsible for handing the memory of a place down through the generations, with or without a Memory Flower.

THE PLACE IN FLOWERS WHERE POLLEN RESTS

Paul West

-

1988

And then, as if heeding the first mesmeric hint of a direction given, he walks back alone, unsteady but tranquil, toward the bed he was conceived in, waiting, if not for doom to crack, at least for the undernourished scurry of its tiny bell.

The title of Paul West's novel also serves as the surname of one of the central figures. George The Place In Flowers Where

Pollen Rests is an old Hopi man living on a mesa in Arizona. His nephew, Oswald Beautiful Badger Going Over The Hill, is the other central figure: a young man who feels disenchanted by Hopi life and decides to try his luck in Hollywood only to fall into pornographic productions. After the accidental death of one of the actresses during a shoot, Oswald returns home. and becomes more connected to both the Hopi way of life and his uncle. But this stability is short-lived. After George dies, the adrift Oswald enlists and serves in Vietnam, an experience which puts him even more at sea. The last lines of the novel see Oswald return to the bed where his life began, waiting for the world to crash in around him one more time.

PALM LATITUDES
Kate Braverman
-
1988

And the earth's heart is beating as it has always, will always, repeating the only word it knows, daughter, daughter, daughter.

At the heart of Kate Braverman's *Palm Latitudes* are three Mexican women in Los Angeles: a sex worker known as La Puta de la Luna, a housewife named Gloria Hernández, and an old witch doctor named Marta Ortega. They are twice removed from society: shunned by the American natives and dismissed by the misogynistic men of their own culture, who seem to believe that the only way to view a woman is as property. Each one of the women struggles, not only for a living, but also for some way to find acceptance in a world that does not allow them their freedom. These three women overlap and separate as they take their different paths: Gloria in anger and madness at her husband's affair, La Puta de la Luna in her removal from those around her, and Marta in her preparations to pass on. The book closes on Marta's death. As she places her face against the earth, she embraces the interconnectedness of all things. The earth seems to embrace the scorned woman and remind her that others' cruel treatment cannot sever her ties to the infinite.

OSCAR AND LUCINDA

Peter Carey

-

1988

Shining fragments of aquarium glass fell like snow around him. And when the long-awaited white fingers of water tapped and lapped on Oscar's lips, he welcomed them in as he always had, with a scream, like a small boy caught in the sheet-folds of a nightmare.

In the mid-19th century Oscar, a minister of the Church of England, meets the eccentric and wealthy glassmaker Lucinda on a boat to Sydney, Australia. Their love of chance leads to many a late-night card game, which results in Oscar's defrocking. As the two grow closer, they decide to build an entire church out of glass from Lucinda's factory, a feat which, amazingly enough, they accomplish. Never one to rest on her laurels, Lucinda bets Oscar that he cannot transport the church from Sydney to Bellingen, a small town which is more than 250 miles away. Ultimately, the trip results in Oscar's death. The last lines contain a dreadful beauty as the cathedral comes crashing down around the disgraced preacher and he is sucked under the waves.

PRISONER'S DILEMMA

Richard Powers

\-

1988

Tell me how free I am.

The prisoner's dilemma is a mathematical model that shows that two rational individuals will resist cooperation, even if it is in their best interest, believing that the other party is destined to betray them. This lack of communication and cooperation is at the heart of Richard Powers's novel. Terminally ill Eddie Hobson, a husband and father to four children, refuses to acknowledge his condition. Instead, Eddie spends his days developing an imaginary world called Hobstown. Within this world of Eddie's creation, people coexist in peace and Walt Disney is a national hero. However, as the truth of his situation begins to set in, the four children, now grown, are forced to return home to be with their ailing father. Just as Eddie was prisoner to the traumas experienced in World War II, so too are his children prisoners to their own histories. Like the prisoner's dilemma, the characters are forced to acknowledge that there is no true way out; their own lack of cooperation has doomed them to the same unescapable ending that was constructed by their own free will.

CAT'S EYE

Margaret Atwood

-

1988

It's old light, and there's not much of it. But it's enough to see by.

Cat's Eye by Margaret Atwood has been called one of the greatest books about adolescent female friendship. Elaine, raised by itinerant parents, forms a close friendship with a group of girls who, upon returning to middle school, begin to bully her incessantly. After they leave Elaine behind in a ravine during winter, Elaine realizes that her relationship with the girls is destructive and cuts ties with them. Upon reentering high school, she recognizes that she has grown stronger than the head girl, Cordelia, and her own self-esteem allows her to start her career as an artist. Meanwhile, Cordelia flunks out of high school and ends up institutionalized. Atwood's honest portrayal of a relationship between the girls culminates with Elaine, older and self-reflective, deciding to rekindle her relationship with Cordelia, though her actions come far too late to reach the troubled woman. The final lines take on a universal scope as even the stars are forced to consider their place in history, their old light shining on both the good and the bad.

BILLY BATHGATE

E. L. Doctorow

-

1989

... And the truckmen in their undershirts unloading their produce, and the horns honking and all the life of the city turning out to greet us just as in the old days of our happiness, before my father fled, when the family used to go walking in this market, this bazaar of life, Bathgate, in the age of Dutch Schultz.

What has come to be considered a classic mafia tale, E. L. Doctorow's *Billy Bathgate* tells the story of 15-year-old Billy Behan, who comes under the wing of big-time Bronx mobster Dutch Schultz. The characters in this story, despite doing wrong, are above all likeable. Though Billy is indoctrinated into the ways of the mob, he eventually finds himself wanting to pursue legitimate business after the death of Schultz and his escape from real-life gangster Lucky Luciano. A year after he separates himself from crime, Billy takes on the care of his infant son, the product of an affair with Dutch's girlfriend, Drew. He commits to raising the child to be good and honorable, and he starts a legitimate business. The last lines echo this calm shift, evoking a simpler time when the neighborhood was full of vibrancy and community.

ARROGANCE
Joanna Scott
-
1990

Egon Schiele in his diary of May 8, 1912:
"Auto-da-fé! Savonarola! Inquisition! Middle Ages!
Castration, hypocrisy!"

Based on the real-life painter Egon Schiele, Joanna Scott's *Arrogance* explores the troubled, obsessive nature of a short-lived artist. Living in Vienna, Austria, from 1890 to 1918, Schiele was an early exponent of expressionistic paintings, twisting his human figures into distorted shapes in order to convey emotion. The fictionalized retelling of his life is done through a handful of voices, including his wife, his mistress, his old friend, and himself. This collection of perspectives creates a portrait of a man not unlike the portraits he himself painted: twisted and disturbed. He wanted to challenge people with his creations, but he himself was far more controversial than his artwork. Jailed for attempting to seduce an underage girl and suspected of painting subjects well below the age of consent, Schiele maintained that people simply could not handle his artistry, or, at least, Joanna Scott's Schiele did. The final lines read as the ravings of a mad man, or the pained cry of a misunderstood visionary. The implications of his declaration are left up to the reader: do we empathize with the creative genius, or scorn him for his twisted view of humanity?

THINGS IN THE NIGHT
Mati Unt
-
1990

We were doomed to die and we were no longer linked to life by any kind of responsibility. We could be as free as the pigs who ran in the field. Those were beautiful years, beautiful autumn days.

Written while Estonia was still under Soviet control, the setting of Mati Unt's *Things in the Night* is hopelessly bleak. However, Unt never lets the text get bogged down in the horrors of life. Instead, his novel approaches the subject of the human condition through absurdity. Various chapters find the narrator rambling for 30 pages as he searches for mushrooms, observing a cannibal diplomatically arguing the merits of cannibalism as he is dragged off to prison, and watering a garden of cacti as the perspective shifts from the narrator to the plants themselves. Traumatic events, such as a life-threatening power outage, are represented through the lens of petty concerns. In the epilogue, the speaker looks back at life under the Soviet regime with a sense of wry nostalgia; there were no expectations and no hope, only the surety of death.

THE LAST MAN STANDING
George Chambers
-
1990

Everyone is waiting for Father, who may,
or may not, come home.

The text of George Chambers's *The Last Man Standing* is arranged into two columns like a play script: on the left are the headings, which act as some of the only directions in the text; on the right are the short paragraphs that correspond to each heading. The narrative follows the son as he returns home to grieve with his troubled family four days after the death of his father. The father, tyrannical from years of military service and awe-inspiring in his grandeur, occupies the back of his son's mind at all times. Within the story are flashes of memories that paint a picture of the father and his family, who are separated by conflicting desires. The final heading, titled "Summer Afternoon," depicts a scene from the past. The children play happily in the backyard as they await the return of their father from work. The family is waiting for the unifying force of the patriarch to return, a futile hope that leaves them just as disconnected from each other as they were at the start.

THE ART LOVER
Carole Maso
-
1990

I put my left hand on his left hand and waved my other hand in front of him and realized that both his eyes were darkened now with his wonderful and perfect sight.

Reality and fiction become increasingly intertwined in Carole Maso's experimental novel *The Art Lover*. Caroline, an artist and author who returns to New York City following her friend's AIDS diagnosis, questions the power of art to help deal with the grief in the world. The novel takes place in three realms: through the eyes of Caroline, through her novel in progress, and finally through the eyes of Maso herself. As Caroline attempts to cope and help her friend through his illness, she becomes reflected in her own novel until the two are inseparable. It becomes clear that, though her life affects her art, her art cannot repair her life in the way she wants it to. As her friend's condition worsens, Caroline is replaced by Maso, sitting by the side of her friend Gary. Gary begins to lose his sight as a result of the disease. Just before he dies he exclaims that he can see again. As Maso waves her hand in front of his eyes, she realizes that his sight is no longer of this world, and perhaps that is for the best.

HARLOT'S GHOST
Norman Mailer
-
1991

TO BE CONTINUED

Like much of Norman Mailer's work, *Harlot's Ghost* blends aspects of reality with entirely fictionalized people and events. Detailing a mostly fictional history of the CIA's involvement with the Cuban Missile Crisis and the assassination of John F. Kennedy, Mailer's nearly 1,200-page book ends with a promise that was never fulfilled. Centered around Harry Hubbard, a clever operative who works at the heart of the CIA while simultaneously orchestrating the agency's downfall, the novel follows a mix of logic and humor as Harry is forced to try and track down a rogue operative who ends up being himself. Sprinkled throughout are side missions and personal dramas that give a sheen of life to the intense and oftentimes paranoid CIA agents. Though he intended to make good on his last line, Mailer never got around to writing a sequel. Still, the self-contained story of Harry Hubbard can stand on its own, and leaves the reader wondering how much they aren't being told.

A THOUSAND ACRES
Jane Smiley
-
1991

This is the gleaming obsidian shard I safeguard above all the others.

Jane Smiley's Pulitzer Prize–winning novel, *A Thousand Acres,* is a modern retelling of Shakespeare's *King Lear.* Larry Cook and his three daughters, Ginny, Rose, and Caroline, live on a large farm in Iowa. Larry decides to turn over the rights to the 1,000-acre farm to his daughters in order to avoid taxes, and the family quickly crumbles. Caroline is cut out of the deal and moves away from the family. Ginny and Rose begin to unravel the darkest corners of their past, not the least of which is the fact that Larry regularly raped them, a fact that Caroline is never made aware of. The characters' descents into madness are far subtler than those in *King Lear,* and the madness is much more modern, with each of the characters slowly losing their marriage and ties to their family as the story unfolds. In the end, we are left with Ginny and her memories, desperately holding the bleak story up to the light in search of a glint of hope.

THE RUNAWAY SOUL
Harold Brodkey
-
1991

Or, rather, let me be quiet in her memory—and in memory of me—for a little while.

Wiley Silenowicz contemplates a childhood of suffering as well as an unhappy first marriage from the contemplative perch of old age in Harold Brodkey's highly anticipated first novel, *The Runaway Soul*. Like all of Brodkey's work, the novel is reminiscent of Proust. Wiley's memories are presented in a stream of consciousness, which results in the time line blurring together, creating a web of events which grows more complex as more thoughts pop into his mind. We shift between thoughts of his budding bisexuality, his abusive relationship with his adopted sister, Nonie, her eventual death, and his years in college. Throughout the novel, Wiley narrates through florid prose that creates a feeling of moving through molasses. Each memory is dragged out across multiple pages, analyzing each second of individual events, a pace that leaves the reader disoriented and wrapped in the general emotion of each scene.

At the end, exhausted from recollection, both Wiley and the reader want a break from the past, and instead settle into the concrete experience of just being.

STRAIGHT OUTTA COMPTON
Ricardo Cortez Cruz
-
1992

"I'm straight outta Compton!" he yelled.

Written using the lingo of early '90s Compton, California, Ricardo Cruz's *Straight Outta Compton* communicates the tension that came to a head during the LA riots of 1992, the same year the book was published. The narrative is disjointed and confusing, mirroring the hectic life of the city. Steeped heavily in the culture of the area, some references to the neighborhood and lifestyle will fly over the heads of unfamiliar readers. Gang violence and misdirected energy fill the pages of the novel, which describes the tragic lives of several Compton teenagers, and ends with the proud exclamation of the city's unofficial slogan.

JESUS' SON
Denis Johnson
-
1992

All these weirdos, and me getting a little better every day right in the midst of them. I had never known, never even imagined for a heartbeat, that there might be a place for people like us.

Denis Johnson's *Jesus' Son* is a collection of short stories that feature a borderline-delusional narrator called Johnathan White, though his true identity is unknown. Throughout the stories, which are not arranged in chronological order, White is frequently high on drugs, nodding off, or scheming for his next fix. He is a tragic character who, in the first story, is at an extremely low point. By the last story, however, he is recovering from his addiction and working at a home for individuals with disabilities, a setting which provides him stability and introduces him to people who make him feel a little bit less alone. While Johnathan still feels separate from the world around him, the ending seems shyly optimistic, a light point in an otherwise turbulent tale.

THE SHIPPING NEWS
E. Annie Proulx
-
1993

For if Jack Buggit could escape from the pickle jar, if a bird with a broken neck could fly away, what else might be possible? Water may be older than light, diamonds crack in hot goat's blood, mountaintops give off cold fire, forests appear in mid-ocean, it may happen that a crab is caught with the shadow of a hand on its back, that the wind be imprisoned in a bit of knotted string. And it may be that love sometimes occurs without pain or misery.

A cold, rocky Newfoundland harbor town is an appropriately harsh setting for E. Annie Proulx's Pulitzer Prize–winning novel, *The Shipping News*. The protagonist, Quoyle, moves to the small Newfoundland town of Killick-Claw with his two daughters after his now-deceased wife attempted to sell the girls into sex slavery. The move serves as a new start for Quoyle and his girls, as well as a way for him to return to his roots. Quoyle struggles against the unforgiving terrain and his own existence, falling in love with a local woman and finding some semblance of peace in the rocky landscape. In the final section, Jack Buggit, a family friend who saved Quoyle from drowning earlier in the book, has drowned in a lobstering accident. During the wake,

Jack miraculously comes back to life, leaving the reader with a false sense of hope. It seems as if the author is reminding us that on the rare occasions when miracles do occur, they will be for someone who is not doomed to misery like Quoyle.

THE FORMS OF WATER
Andrea Barrett
-
1993

The colors seemed very bright against the mist, and through the air, so softly we could not be sure we heard it, came the sound of the men chanting to welcome in the night.

Andrea Barrett's *The Forms of Water* is a fictional account of the construction of the Quabbin Reservoir in western Massachusetts. Brendan Auberon, an 80-year-old former monk, is a man whose home was lost when his town was flooded to build the reservoir. His final wish is to make the journey to the reservoir to see his hometown one more time. After convincing his middle-aged nephew Henry to steal a nursing home van, the two set out with Henry's younger sister, Wiloma, and her daughter, Wendy. All four characters are at very different places in their lives, yet they are connected through their loneliness. Though a van full of conflicting personalities may sound like a road trip cliché, their story is nothing short of an awakening, one that can only occur when the present meets the past. At the end of each chapter is a letter from Henry's great-grandfather protesting the flooding of the town. In the final lines, there is an almost spiritual quality to visiting the past, one that has a lasting impact on the present and the future.

THE VIRGIN SUICIDES
Jeffrey Eugenides
-
1993

It didn't matter in the end how old they had been, or that they were girls, but only that we had loved them, and that they hadn't heard us calling, still do not hear us, up here in the tree house, with our thinning hair and soft bellies, calling them out of those rooms where they went to be alone for all time, alone in suicide, which is deeper than death, and where we will never find the pieces to put them back together.

Told from the perspective of a group of anonymous boys, Jeffrey Eugenides's *The Virgin Suicides* contemplates the suicide of five young sisters. Now grown men, these unnamed narrators pore over the events that led to the five girls taking their own lives, trying desperately to make sense of the mystery which continues to plague them. Having once lived in the same neighborhood as Cecilia, Lux, Bonnie, Mary, and Therese, the boys became fascinated by the enigmatic family. After Cecilia flings herself out of a second-story window during a party celebrating her return from the hospital after a failed suicide attempt, the family becomes reclusive. A year later, after being invited over to the house one night by Lux, the boys discover that the four remaining girls are also suicidal. Three of the sisters are successful in their suicide attempts, and Mary, the sole surviving sister, kills herself one month later. Horrified, the boys are unable to comprehend the actions of the girls. In the end, they must accept that the girls' personal depression is beyond their reach. No matter how much they cared about them, sometimes it takes more than just love to reach into the interior of a person.

HEADHUNTER
Timothy Findley
-
1993

It's only a book, they would say. That's all it is. A story. Just a story.

In Timothy Findley's *Headhunter*, a schizophrenic spiritualist named Lilah Kemp lives in a dystopian Toronto. Lilah, imbued with powers she has little to no control over, accidentally manifests a physical embodiment of Kurtz from Joseph Conrad's *Heart of Darkness*. Fearing that the powerful villain will thrive in the chaotic Toronto climate, Lilah sets off to find Charles Marlow, the protagonist of Conrad's story, to defeat Kurtz. Instead of the rivers of Africa, Kurtz exercises his cruel power over Toronto's Parkin Institute of Psychiatry, where Lilah is a patient. In the end, Marlow does appear to thwart Kurtz, and good triumphs over evil. But things in Toronto are so hopeless that Lilah believes this victory will be dismissed as nothing more than fiction.

BLUESMAN
Andre Dubus III

—

1993

And he hoped they would wake him in time to swing his legs over the bedside in the near-dark, to be sitting straight and ready as Jim's alarm went off, and his bedsprings squeaked, and Leo heard his father, coming for him.

Leo Suthur, the protagonist of Andre Dubus III's novel *Bluesman*, is 17 years old. It is the summer of 1967 in Massachusetts, and he is trying to squeeze everything he can out of the few months before he turns 18. He is tangled in a mesh of interpersonal relationships that include his girlfriend, her communist father, his own distant, but caring father, and his mother, who communicates to him through letters written before her death. Leo's need to live as much as he can while he can fills the novel with verve and perspective. In the last lines, on the night before Leo is shipped off to fight in Vietnam, he lays in bed, listening to the ringing in his ears from a blues show he played in with his father. He hears the silence of the woods and the river out his window, and he wishes dearly that he will wake up before his dad's alarm so that he might appreciate the stillness one last time before reality comes crashing in.

IN A COUNTRY OF MOTHERS
A. M. Homes
-
1993

She turned on a lamp, checked her appointment book, sorted the magazines in the waiting room, refilled the Kleenex supply, plumped the pillows on her sofa, and then sat down in her chair, ready.

A. M. Homes's *In a Country of Mothers* explores the murky world of professionalism among doctors and patients, as well as the identity issues that arise from not knowing one's past. Claire, the central character of the narrative, is a successful Manhattan therapist with a family. However, when a young patient by the name of Jody reveals that she is an adopted child, Claire becomes obsessed with the daughter she gave up for adoption. Perhaps, she thinks, she is Jody. As Claire becomes more infatuated with the idea that Jody is her daughter, she becomes increasingly more inappropriate, crossing countless ethical boundaries. Her role as an objective third party is shattered as she inserts herself into Jody's life and ignores her own family. Whether or not the two are related becomes irrelevant as Claire becomes more obsessive. Eventually, after the twisted relationship culminates in a frantic exchange, Claire resigns herself to leave Jody alone. She thinks that, in time, Jody will come to her, and tidies up her office, still very much in the throes of denial.

THE EYE IN THE DOOR
Pat Barker
-
1993

"There'll always be an England," he told him and ran, laughing, down the steps.

The second installment in Pat Barker's Regeneration trilogy, *The Eye in the Door* continues the story of Billy Prior, a soldier undergoing treatment for shell shock in World War I. The underlying focus of the narrative is on double lives and secret identities. As Billy Prior continues to conceal his class origins from the Ministry of Munition he serves in, so too does the aristocratic Charles Manning, a fellow soldier, conceal his homosexuality. In the end, Billy turns down a permanent job with the Ministry to return to his home, embracing his identity at last. The last lines hold a sense of joviality, as Billy leaves England, and his false self, behind, fully aware that there will always be duality as long as humanity exists.

GOING NATIVE
Stephen Wright
-
1994

There was only the Viewer, slumped forever in his sour seat, the bald shells of his eyes boiling in pictures, a biblical flood of them, all saturated tones and deep focus, not one life-size, and the hands applauding, always applauding, palms abraded to an open fretwork of gristle and bone, the ruined teeth fixed in a yellowy smile that will not diminish, that will not fade, he's happy, he's being entertained.

Stephen Wright's *Going Native* is a surrealistic portrait of the 20th-century American landscape. The novel opens on a barbecue, with two couples shooting the breeze over dinner until one of the men, Wylie, takes us on a tour of the country. Though it is not always explicitly stated that the narrative is following Wylie, the rage-filled night in which Wylie steals and murders to his heart's delight is the thread holding the narrative together. He is a killer gone berserk, journeying across America in a Ford Galaxy. From Chicago to Vegas, he travels unnoticed as each location brings about a new facet of the American Dream for him to kill and unceremoniously abandon as we move on to the next chapter. Eventually, his grand tour ends. As he sits in his car, delirious from insomnia and confused as to which personality is his own, Wylie is no longer a participant in the narrative. He has become numbed to the horror of his own destruction and is simply entertained, a sobering portrait of modern life.

IN THE LAKE OF THE WOODS
Tim O'Brien
-
1994

Could the truth be so simple? So terrible?

Tim O'Brien's novel *In the Lake of the Woods* presents readers with a plethora of details surrounding the disappearance of a woman named Kathy Wade, and explicitly leaves it up to them to decide what happened to her. The story is told through the eyes of her husband, John, and follows a nonlinear time line. John is a failed politician whose involvement in a massacre of innocent civilians in Vietnam sunk his Congressional campaign. The story is told in flashbacks, all the way from his childhood to his time in Vietnam, as well as in testimony from those involved in the political campaign. As John's violent tendencies become clear, a sense of unease surrounds the search for his wife. At the end of the novel, several plausible answers to the question of Kathy's disappearance are offered: she may have accidentally drowned, she may have been killed by John, or the couple may have planned it together, hoping to start a new life in Canada. This final, happy ending is what O'Brien is calling us to consider at the end, challenging us to move past the pessimism that is slowly clouding our perception.

THE WIND-UP BIRD CHRONICLE
Haruki Murakami
-
1995

"In a place far away from anyone or anywhere, I drifted off for a moment."

The original Japanese edition of Haruki Murakami's *The Wind-Up Bird Chronicle* was initially published as three separate books. The popular, unconventional novel tells the story of Toru Okada, a man who sets out to find his cat and ends up finding—and losing—much more. Toru navigates both mundane and extraordinary situations, all the while seeming to be in a dreamlike state of consciousness, with one foot in reality and the other in a timeless space. Past, present, and future intertwine as Toru continues searching for his pet and his estranged wife. Eventually, his search leads him to an illusory reality hidden at the bottom of a well. After delving deeper and deeper into the bottomless well of different realities,

Toru finally drifts from his dreamlike lucidity to peaceful slumber, if even just for a moment.

PHOSPHOR IN DREAMLAND
Rikki Ducornet
-
1995

And that pulsing behind her, close upon the twin orbs of her bountiful posterior, kneeled a great beaked figure—an enigmatic lôplôp . . .

Structured as a series of letters from one friend to another, Rikki Ducornet's *Phosphor in Dreamland* tells the story of a fictional island called Birdland, a now-vanished country inhabited by spectacular flora and fauna. In these letters, the narrator describes the pursuit of Phosphor, an inventor with a clubfoot, to document the wonderful birds of the island using a *camera obscura* of his own invention. The letters convey a yearning for a seemingly magical land destroyed by colonialism. Throughout Phosphor's search for the lôplôp, the large bird that is nearly extinct due to overhunting, he realizes that there is no true way to preserve a memory in a way that lasts through time. Once a thing has been destroyed, it cannot be fully restored. Instead, it is the job of those who remember to keep the past alive through their art. In the final lines, the speaker sees, at last, the bird he

has been so desperate to find, and by doing so keeps a sliver of
Birdland alive in the minds of the readers.

PAINTED DESERT

Frederick Barthelme

-

1995

---

*For a minute all I could think of was what we must
look like from the sky, the black Lincoln, the two
splintered headlights shooting into nothing, the two
taillights glowing red tracers behind us, the big flat
space everywhere and all this dust swelling around us
like a land-speed record attempt. We rocketed across
that desert sand.*

Frederick Barthelme's *Painted Desert* sets out to critique the
fatalist frenzy of self-proclaimed internet saviors. Del Tribune,
in the throes of a midlife crisis, sets out on a trip from his small
town with his 27-year-old internet-obsessed girlfriend, Jen, her
father, and her friend Penny. The group's goal is to find justice
for a single victim of the LA riots, which took place years prior
to the novel. When Jen's barrage of rage-filled emails stirs up
a violent activist, the four characters realize they may need
to rethink their approach to social change. In the end, the
adventurers take on a mind-set of appreciation for the simple

beauty of nature and the ability of people to connect personally over violent chance. As the frame widens to portray this perspective in the final scene, the reader is left with the warmth of the characters' personal relationships in the face of blissful insignificance.

THE END OF THE STORY
Lydia Davis
-
1995

And since all along there had been too many ends to the story, and since they did not end anything, but only continued something, something not formed into any story, I needed an act of ceremony to end the story.

Lydia Davis's *The End of the Story* follows an unnamed woman's attempts to forget a past love affair, one that ended in emotional turmoil and insecurity. The unnamed woman attempts to move on by writing down the details she can recall. Skewed by the inaccuracy of memory, the portrait she paints of her lover resembles that of a character rather than the individual. The woman hopes that, by placing the memories within a structured narrative, she will be able to rid herself of the obsession. It is for this reason that she turns the simple act of drinking a cup of tea in a bookstore into something of ceremonial significance, as it is the one thing she can cling to in the aftermath of the relationship. In a story of endings, both of relationships and seasons of life, the final ending has a meditative quality to it, a closure that stills the reader much like a cup of tea.

SABBATH'S THEATER
Philip Roth
-
1995

And he couldn't do it. He could not fucking die. How could he leave? How could he go? Everything he hated was here.

Mickey Sabbath, the titular character of Philip Roth's *Sabbath's Theater*, is a depraved, disgusting, and evil individual who goes beyond the traditional antihero in more ways than one. In a way, he is also an anti-villain: a man selfish enough to be detested but pathetic enough to elicit some amount of pity from the reader. Even as the aging, failed puppeteer harasses young women, betrays his wife and friends, and masturbates on graves, readers still find themselves feeling a kind of twisted sympathy for Sabbath. By the end, the suicidal Sabbath finds himself unable to commit to his own death and is instead released back to the world at large. Sabbath seems too dark a man to be allowed the respite of death; he is sentenced to torment at the hands of life itself, separated from all he once held dear. A fitting end for the not-quite-villain.

THE GREEN MILE
Stephen King
-
1996

*We each owe a death, there are no exceptions,
I know that, but sometimes, oh God, the Green
Mile is so long.*

Originally published in six separate volumes, *The Green Mile* has become one of Stephen King's most beloved novels. Though the story does employ magic realism, it does not feature as many fantastical elements as the majority of King's works. The book tells the story of prison block supervisor Paul Edgecombe and various prisoners on "the Green Mile," the nickname for death row at the Cold Mountain Penitentiary. One such prisoner, named John Coffey, possesses supernatural powers that allow him to heal living things and is unnaturally empathetic. As the inmates wait for their eventual execution, it becomes clear to Paul that Coffey is innocent of the crimes he was charged with. Coffey, overwhelmed by the cruelty of the world, comforts Paul before his own execution, as he is ready to be free of human suffering. In the last lines, Paul thinks back to the events of the Green Mile from a nursing home, he himself now waiting for the final embrace of death. The haunting last lines echo the idea that, no matter how innocent, death always comes to collect.

INFINITE JEST
David Foster Wallace
-
1996

And when he came back to, he was flat on his back on the beach in the freezing sand, and it was raining out of a low sky, and the tide was way out.

David Foster Wallace's 1,000-page postmodern classic *Infinite Jest* took the literary world by storm. The encyclopedic novel takes place in a highly detailed future world in which the United States, Mexico, and Canada have formed into one nation, and corporate sponsors dictate many aspects of everyday life. Famous for its numerous interwoven narratives and heavy reliance upon endnotes, the complex stories loosely orbit around a videotape called "Infinite Jest," which is so addictive that the viewer is unable to avert their eyes, resulting in their eventual death. The story is told using postmodernist and pop themes, embracing the idea of a nonlinear story line in its exploration of the numbing desire for happiness that permeates contemporary America. In the end, despite the chaos that makes up the narrative, we return to the past for a brief moment, giving the reader a glimpse of natural beauty in the face of the impending rise of entertainment and megamedia.

THE RETURN OF PAINTING, THE PEARL, AND ORION: A TRILOGY
Leslie Scalapino
-
1997

. . . Out walking by magnolia blossoms cups and entirely inside as there is no sense of there being anything in there.

Orion is the final work in Leslie Scalapino's collection *The Return of Painting, The Pearl, and Orion: A Trilogy*. Primarily a poet, it is no surprise that Scalapino's novels are less than traditional. The novels in the trilogy feature constantly shifting viewpoints and text that focuses on aesthetics rather than stories. She does not hold the hands of her readers; her prose, like her poetry, is meant to create a reaction that is entirely subjective, while also conveying a disjointed plot that consists of textual bursts describing a chaotic reality. Twisting words to create portraits of characters that are felt if not fully understood, Scalapino's work intentionally resists the formation of a comprehensive plot line, instead capturing seemingly unrelated events in a bewildering tapestry of flowing language. The closing line, like many of those that precede it, could come from the perspective of any man, woman, or child on earth, allowing the reader to slip into the novel and smell the magnolia blossoms.

UNDERWORLD
Don DeLillo
-
1997

Peace.

Often considered Don DeLillo's masterpiece, *Underworld* captures an ever-changing America during the second half of the 20th century. Nick Shay, a young Bronx native, is just one of the many characters who carry us through the decades covered by this sprawling narrative. Bouncing between different years and different stories, many of which combine elements of reality and fiction, the book weaves history together with more vibrancy than any American history textbook. Beginning at the infamous Dodgers-Giants playoff for the 1951 National League pennant, the story loosely follows the home run baseball hit by Bobby Thomson as it spirals toward the future. Here, DeLillo describes a world that exists entirely in cyberspace; everything is linked together, and everything is at peace. Or perhaps it is simply a future imagined.

DRA—

Stacey Levine

-

1997

He fell back into the net, which rocked imperceptibly above them, and he sang quietly to himself, as if that helped him negotiate his exhaustion.

Dra—, the title character of Stacey Levine's first novel, is on a seemingly endless quest for employment. As she navigates through the strange, terminal-like setting of the story, she becomes increasingly dissatisfied and maddened by the banality of the opportunities with which she is presented. Her most notable career options are to either research dust or monitor a water pump. It is through these roles that the characters establish their own identities. The inhabitants of this world have accepted the tedium of their jobs; they have become numb to the illness-inducing effects of nonstop work and have essentially lost their minds. Dra—, however, cannot accept her fate. She puts off work time and time again, desperate for another option. In the end, it seems, we learn that everyone is working for their own insignificant momentary escapes, oblivious to the self-propelled exhaustion that will inevitably end in their death.

MEMOIRS OF A GEISHA
Arthur Golden
-
1997

Whatever our struggles and triumphs, however we may suffer them, all too soon they bleed into a wash, just like watery ink on paper.

Arthur Golden's *Memoirs of a Geisha* provides a detailed look at how World War II not only affected Japan as a nation, but also geisha in particular. Chiyo Sakamoto, the novel's protagonist, serves as the book's narrator. Separated from her family and only shown kindness once during a chance meeting with the Chairman, Chiyo spends most of her life stoically fighting against poverty and working to regain her own agency. Through diplomatic connections and careful training, Chiyo (renamed Sayuri) becomes a desired and accomplished geisha. Her prowess as a geisha and her sociopolitical contacts allow her to escape World War II unharmed after the closure of her geisha house and reconnect with the love of her life, the Chairman. In the end, it is her measured stoicism that gives her the strength to endure whatever happens, be it war, poverty, or simply life, because she knows eventually everything fades.

PANTHER IN THE BASEMENT
Amos Oz
-
1997

Have I betrayed them all again by telling the story? Or is it the other way around: would I have betrayed them if I had not told it?

Set just outside Jerusalem in 1947 during the last year of British occupation, Amos Oz's *Panther in the Basement* follows a 12-year-old boy nicknamed Proffy. Proffy is the leader of an imaginary Israeli resistance operation called the FOD: Freedom or Death. After he is apprehended by a British police officer named Sergeant Dunlop for playing past curfew, the two form an unlikely friendship, with Dunlop giving Proffy English lessons on a regular basis while Proffy teaches Dunlop modern Hebrew. This causes Proffy to rethink his previously intractable hatred of the British people. Proffy, who narrates the story as an adult, seems to have never decided where he belonged in the world: as a firmly loyal soldier of the resistance, or as someone whose interests are free to wander elsewhere. He seems to pose his final questions as much to himself as he does to the reader, trying to weigh the cost of public and private betrayal in the face of history.

BROKEBACK MOUNTAIN
E. Annie Proulx
-
1997

There was some open space between what he knew and what he tried to believe, but nothing could be done about it, and if you can't fix it you've got to stand it.

E. Annie Proulx's short story *Brokeback Mountain* flips stereotypical expectations on their head. By presenting Ennis del Mar and Jack Twist, two hard-nosed cowboys, in a homosexual relationship, Proulx plays with societal perceptions of traditional manliness and the American farmhand. Her use of character types that are not directly associated with homosexuality gives the relationship a welcome air of normalcy, one that is rejected by the world around them. The two men continue their relationship past their time on Brokeback Mountain, engaging in extramarital affairs that eventually lead to Ennis's divorce from his wife. After Jack's death, Ennis is left with only the memory of their love for one another. There is a twist of tenderness and resentment in the final lines, as Ennis cannot simply show his love like the generations who have come before him: he must stand by his love and wait for the world to judge them.

CHARMING BILLY
Alice McDermott
-
1997

As if, in that wide-ranging anthology of stories that was the lives of the saints—that was, as well, my father's faith and Billy's and some part of my own— what was actual, as opposed to what was imagined, as opposed to what was believed, made, when you got right down to it, any difference at all.

Often considered her masterpiece, Alice McDermott's *Charming Billy* opens following Billy's death, an event that deeply affects all who knew him. While it is clear that Billy drank himself to death, how such a lovable man ended up in that position is unknown to both the reader and Billy's cousin Dennis's daughter, who acts as the narrator of this story. Upon the shocking realization that Dennis lied to Billy about the death of his childhood sweetheart, Eva, the narrator embarks on a journey to learn the true nature of Billy's life. Along the way, the various tales of Billy and the town become jumbled by different perspectives, until the narrator realizes that there is no such thing as a true account of a person. She ends up with an image of Billy that is as true as it needs to be, one that neither deifies nor damns the man, but instead takes him as he is, flaws and all. In the end, we get the impression that it is not the accuracy of Billy's history that defines him, rather it is the shards of the "true" Billy aggregated from each story that is the real continuation of his legacy.

MEMORIES OF MY FATHER WATCHING TV
Curtis White
-
1998

"Nothin'."

Curtis White's *Memories of My Father Watching TV* is narrated by Chris, a now-grown man who recalls his father with a humor that masks loss. Chris can only remember his dad as a man who, despite his children's best efforts, was always glued to the television set. Each chapter is framed in the style of a different television show of the time, from corny sitcoms and quiz shows, to cowboy dramas and the Kitchen Debate between Vice President Richard Nixon and Soviet premier Nikita Khrushchev. These recollections are framed by what Chris wishes his dad provided, ranging from affection to basic conversation. In the end, Chris's father is a bare shell of a man, and the reader must come to the same conclusion as Chris: whatever his father should have been to him, he is nothing now.

NOBODY'S GIRL
Antonya Nelson
-
1998

In her mind's eye, she could clearly see Luziana as she'd been then, when her baby lived inside her, when she still attended school, sitting in her melancholy pose, lifting the massive, overwhelming anthology, her skinny arm a mere flower stem, weak under the weight of all those sad stories.

Antonya Nelson's *Nobody's Girl* follows a character who, like many people, feels her life is being wasted in a place that does not challenge her intellectually. Living in the small southwestern town of Pinetop, New Mexico, Birdy Stone is an unsatisfied teacher nearing her 30s. Birdy is a woman who ran away from her once-stable life in order to find adventure. Instead, all she found was a life that is far from those in her favorite stories. Birdy shoplifts with a fellow teacher, pursues a sexual relationship with a teenager, and takes on a job writing about a mysterious death in order to try and add variety to her day-to-day routine, but she can never escape the boredom of her interior life. In the end, she finds herself thinking about Luziana, a student who spent her time bettering herself instead of chasing after drama. In the last lines, the reader gets the sense that, while Luziana may not have been happy, she was far more content than Birdy could ever hope to be.

MOTHERLESS BROOKLYN
Jonathan Lethem
-
1999

Tell your story walking.

Set in his hometown of Brooklyn, Jonathan Lethem's novel *Motherless Brooklyn* tells the story of Lionel Essrog, a 1950s private detective with Tourette's syndrome. Essrog becomes wrapped up in a new case when his mentor and father figure, Frank Minna, is mysteriously stabbed to death. In a novel that takes the traditional murder mystery hard-boiled detective case and uses it as an ironic backdrop, the cast of unique characters are allowed their own personalities and struggles. Essrog's tics both aid and frustrate his detective work, and his involuntary exclamations break through the charismatic reserve that is typical of the genre. This novel is as much a love letter to New York as it is to the black-and-white film noir genre that it emulates. It is fitting that the closing line is an expression that Minna was so keen on—one which affirms the fast-paced attitude of the big city and expresses the need to tell one's story, no matter how cliché or roundabout it may be

THE AMAZING ADVENTURES
OF KAVALIER & CLAY
Michael Chabon
-
2000

When Rosa and Joe picked it up they saw that Sammy had taken a pen and, bearing down, crossed out the name of the never-more-than-theoretical family that was printed above the address, and in its place written, sealed in a neat black rectangle, knotted by the stout cord of an ampersand, the words KAVALIER & CLAY.

Jewish history, World War II, and the golden age of comic books are just a few of the topics explored in Michael Chabon's Pulitzer Prize–winning novel, *The Amazing Adventures of Kavalier & Clay*. Two cousins, Josef Kavalier and Sammy Klayman, meet each other in their late teens and immediately recognize a shared interest in creating comics: Josef is an incredible illustrator and Sammy a gifted writer. They achieve astronomical success with their character, the Escapist, who acts as an embodiment of Josef's love for fantastic escapes and his desperate need to save his family from the Nazi regime. Josef abandons his girlfriend to serve overseas, leading Sammy to step into the Kavalier household in Josef's place. Josef returns, but Sammy is outed as a gay man on public television and flees the Kavalier and Clay household in the middle of the night. In the final lines, Sammy leaves one last reminder of where their journey began: "KAVALIER & CLAY."

PORTRAIT OF AN ARTIST, AS AN OLD MAN

Joseph Heller

-

2000

He was not surprised, and he began to think seriously of writing the book you've just read.

Joseph Heller's final work, *Portrait of an Artist, as an Old Man*, could be read autobiographically. The protagonist, Eugene Pota, cannot seem to create a work of fiction which matches the quality of his earlier works, a situation which Heller himself struggled with following his immensely successful *Catch-22*. The book contains a variety of writings which Pota started but never finished, including a monologue by Hera about Zeus's infidelity, and a meditation on his own wife's sex life. But these stories always succumb to writer's block and self-doubt before they can become more than just ideas. Through Pota, Heller creates a caricature of the writer fretting over his legacy, a man who considers writing but rarely does, a husk of potential that never moves beyond the sudden spark of inspiration into the hard work of writing. In the last lines, Pota realizes that his experience of not writing can become his next story, a revelation that, we feel, may get him nowhere. Unlike Pota, however, Heller knows his legacy will remain intact; he simply wishes to have one last bit of satirical fun before he goes.

BLONDE
Joyce Carol Oates
-
2000

"Norma Jean—see? That man is your father."

Joyce Carol Oates's historical novel *Blonde* explores the inner life of Marilyn Monroe, born Norma Jean, one of America's biggest stars. The work is a fictionalized account, but it is so widely read and revered that some consider it an unofficial biography despite the many obvious diversions from the facts. Norma's life begins with the instability of her mother, committed to a mental institution after being poisoned by chemicals at her workplace. Norma becomes a whirlwind of tragedy, scandal, and sexual encounters tinted by a grimy reality that gives dimension to America's favorite actress. The largest deviation from reality is the ending, which presents Norma's death by poison at the hands of John F. Kennedy's hired hit man in an eerie echo of her mother's fate. The book ends as Norma finally meets her father and regains her human identity outside of the spotlight of fame.

BY NIGHT IN CHILE
Roberto Bolaño
-
2000

And then the storm of shit begins.

The entirety of Roberto Bolaño's novella *By Night in Chile* consists of only two paragraphs: the first comprises the first 130 pages, and the second is made up of one final line. The story takes place over one night as the dying Father Urrutia narrates his life story to the reader. Through the monologue format, Bolaño is able to comprehensively discuss weighty topics, such as religion, politics, and art over a brief period of time, introducing new metaphors and analogies to the reader as he moves on to the next topic. Able to balance the fervor of religion with the tumultuous political climate of

Chile, the nontraditional format gives the impression of a life happening all at once. The story ends with Father Urrutia, a failed poet, realizing that his religious tenets were flawed, and that he directly contributed to the rise of fascism in Chile. The paragraph of his old life breaks, and a new paragraph begins, just as the consequences of his actions are realized by both him and the reader.

WHITE TEETH
Zadie Smith
-
2000

Archie, for one, watched the mouse. He watched it stand very still for a second with a smug look as if it expected nothing less. He watched it scurry away, over his hand. He watched it dash along the table and through the hands of those who wished to pin it down. He watched it leap off the end and disappear through an air vent. Go on my son! thought Archie.

Zadie Smith's debut novel, *White Teeth,* chronicles the lives of two friends who fought alongside each other in World War II. The protagonists, Samad Iqbal and Archie Jones, are friends despite their dedication to different ideals, Samad to Islam and Archie to a banal everyday life. The novel concludes with the escape of FutureMouse, an impressive and diabolical genetically modified creature who represents the cure to life-threatening diseases. In the end, Archie, who has been a rather boring, complacent character throughout the novel, dives in front of a bullet in an entirely uncharacteristic moment of heroism. As FutureMouse's cage crashes to the floor, Archie watches the rodent escape, feeling a swell of pride that this creation can leave behind the society that he himself has become entrenched in.

THE FINAL COUNTRY
James Crumley
-
2001

But wherever my final country is, my ashes will go back to Montana when I die. Maybe I've stopped looking for love. Maybe not. Maybe I will go to Paris. Who knows? But I'll sure as hell never go back to Texas again.

The trope of the hard-drinking, drug-using antihero private detective is alive and well in *The Final Country*, James Crumley's fourth and final novel featuring Milo Milodragovitch, a 60-year-old war veteran turned private investigator whose moral code does not fall in line with that of conventional society. Milodragovitch sets out to prove the innocence of

Enos Walker, a man with a laundry list of supposed crimes that slowly transform Milodragovitch's small Texan community. The decades-long saga of Milodragovitch comes to a relatively happy end in *The Final Country* as he contemplates a future outside of the state that fueled his many demons. Sick of the subterfuge and slander of wealthy landowners seeking to maintain the illusion of normalcy, Milodragovitch is content to leave the madness in Texas.

REQUIEM
Curtis White
-
2001

What doesn't leave, though, is this beautiful little feeling about a dog, a boat, a sunset, and a superb sense of forgiveness.

In typical avant-garde fashion, Curtis White's postmodern *Requiem* challenges readers to appreciate the novel as a piece of art rather than just a story. White's book is divided up into six sections, each containing various modes of storytelling, from email correspondences with a porn star to random notes and interviews between the wandering Modern Prophet and a series of individuals who appear more and more depraved as the novel goes on. Without a traceable plot, the novel is dominated by thematic patterns, such as the juxtaposition of modern pornographic indulgences and biblical tales and the desperation for attention in the face of the internet. Witness to the societal decay is man's best friend, who suffers as an unwilling party in our ever-worsening disassociation with life. In the end, the turbulent barrage of scenes comes to a rest at last, as the reader appreciates the natural, unhurried beauty of a simpler time.

FIXER CHAO

Han Ong

-

2001

But apart from seeing Jokey again, my life remained
an uninflected one of stalking around unbothered,
until finally one day a thought succeeded in forming
itself: that what had been a lifelong irritant–that I
walked around the world unseen, as if invisible–had
now become a strange and beautiful blessing, freeing
me to live my life all over again, as if the previous
one had only been a rough draft, a vague outline to
be crossed over, exceeded, to be transcended, as if that
life was the earthly life and this one, the California
one, with myself benumbed and calm and floating
inside the bubble of mall after white mall–places
that were like hospitals with their piped-in music
and blanching light–as if this life, finally, was the
heavenly one.

In *Fixer Chao*, Han Ong explores the world of the outsider. The main character, William Narciso Paulinha, is a gay Filipino hustler on the streets of New York. Under the guidance of his newfound friend Shem, William poses as a Chinese guru and master in the art of feng shui, a skill which he uses to rearrange the homes of Manhattan socialites to influence their fate.

William is able to elude suspicion because the ignorant men and women of the upper class assume that he possesses the mystical powers which he flaunts. Eventually, though, his scheming catches up to him, and his constructed life unravels. William receives death threats, Shem turns the story of the phony feng shui master into a book, and William flees to Los Angeles. His status as an outsider presents him with the opportunity to start over, as the invisibility he once loathed now allows him to slip under the radar.

AUNT RACHEL'S FUR
Raymond Federman
-
2001

*Good bye, my friend, take it easy, and as we say in America when starting a new life, **wish me luck** . . .*

In his experimental novel *Aunt Rachel's Fur*, Raymond Federman plays with chronology, pulling his story together out of an intricate quilt of snippets and monologues. Reymond Namredef, the protagonist of the novel, is a French expatriate and aspiring author. After having lived unhappily in America for 10 years, he returns to France to pursue his dream of being a writer. He meets a man in a café who claims to be a "professional listener." With no discernable order or continuity, Namredef tells his life story to the man. The narrative must be taken with a grain of salt, as Namredef is not averse to telling a fib or two. When all is said and done, the listener reveals himself as none other than Raymond Federman, or at least a fictionalized version of him. The novel deploys the autobiographical format satirically, as the two same-named characters talk at each other over their own history. This creates a spiraling narrative that includes nontraditional text placement and tangential plot points. In the end, Namredef bids Federman adieu and sets out to start a new life, one undoubtedly full of hyperbole.

THE CORRECTIONS

Jonathan Franzen

-

2OO1

She was seventy-five and she was going to make some changes in her life.

Many readers are of the opinion that the final line of Jonathan Franzen's *The Corrections* must be taken with a grain of salt. Enid, who is finally free of her husband, Alfred, after years of being held back by his burgeoning dementia, can finally lead the life she has always wanted to at the young age of 75. Enid has lived out her one goal: get the children home for Christmas. Yet the larger cast of nuclear family members are still falling apart in one way or another. The eldest is a depressive materialist with a developing drinking problem, the middle child is running an internet scam in Lithuania, and the youngest lost her job after having an affair with both her boss and her boss's wife. Nothing about this family is up to code, and their lives steadily fall apart until Alfred succumbs to his disease. Alfred's institutionalization is an odd turning point for the family, as they pick up the pieces of their lives and start anew. In a vacuum, this certainly sounds like a happy ending, but the story has set us up to be skeptical. However, the last lines may be sincere in this otherwise cynical family drama; perhaps Franzen, after stripping these characters of their phony, midwestern facade, finally allows the matriarch to build her own identity, separate from her family.

LIFE OF PI
Yann Martel
-
2001

Very few castaways can claim to have survived so long at sea as Mr. Patel, and none in the company of an adult Bengal tiger.

Rarely does the final line of a novel sum up the narrative so succinctly. But *Life of Pi*, the best-selling novel by Yann Martel, is no typical work of fiction. Right up until the very end, the reader is still left questioning whether or not the events of this castaway journey took place exactly as young Pi Patel described them. It is, after all, unlikely that a boy could happily coexist on a lifeboat with a tiger. It is more likely that his tale of human depravity and cannibalism at the hands of the boat's French cook is the real truth. In this sense, the closing line accomplishes two seemingly contradictory things: it reaffirms the truth of the book's events, while highlighting the unlikeliness of the situation. Above all, though, it shows the power a story can possess. Perhaps young Pi does fabricate a tale of adventure and spirituality in order to cope with a horrifying reality. The final lines give the reader space for this interpretation, allowing them, too, to find comfort from humanity's dark side in Pi's story, real or not.

MIDDLESEX
Jeffrey Eugenides
-
2002

I lost track after a while, happy to be home, weeping for my father, and thinking about what was next.

Jeffrey Eugenides's Pulitzer Prize–winning book *Middlesex* tells the story of Cal (born Caliope) a Greek American intersex individual who is raised as a girl but later identifies as a man.

In the novel, the specific gene that causes the development of both female and male traits is followed from a small Asia Minor village through America and finally to Berlin, where Cal narrates the story of his life and family. In a unique tale of heritage and identity, we follow Cal as he struggles with his sexuality, gender, and identity. As Cal returns home for his father's funeral, he learns that his grandparents were brother and sister, a secret only he and his grandparents know. Armed with a better understanding of his own history, Cal reinserts himself into his family. In the last lines, Cal takes on the role of the man of the house, mourning his lost father while celebrating his own return home.

THE LOVELY BONES
Alice Sebold
-
2002

I wish you all a long and happy life.

Alice Sebold's *The Lovely Bones* is narrated from heaven by the 14-year-old victim of rape and murder, a girl named Susie Salmon. We follow Susie, her family, and the detective trying to solve her murder at the hands of their neighbor, Mr. Harvey. Through a journey of grief and acceptance, Susie is able to move from her own personal heaven to the larger heaven in the sky, and her family moves on. The novel ends with a certain kind of closure, though not one expected by most. Susie's bones are not found, and the killer is not brought to justice. Instead, he dies in a freak accident involving an icicle while attempting to kill another girl. Still, the book closes with a feeling of contentment as we watch Susie's loved ones rebuild their lives. In the final line, Susie bids the reader farewell as she accepts her death, finally at peace.

INFLATING A DOG: THE STORY OF ELLA'S LUNCH LAUNCH

Eric Kraft

-

2002

"Well," I said, "let me tell you," and I told them a briefer, simpler version of the story I have just told you, and while I was telling it, my mother, Ella, who for one unforgettable summer ran Ella's Lunch Launch, died.

Peter Leroy is the central figure of Eric Kraft's *The Personal History, Adventures, Experiences and Observations of Peter Leroy*. In one volume of the saga, *Inflating a Dog: The Story of Ella's Lunch Launch*, Peter Leroy helps his mother, Ella, enact a plan to operate a Long Island cruising vessel to rope summer visitors into spending a little bit of extra money on a tour of the town. Peter notices that the boat is leaking heavily, so every night he goes to the dock and pumps the water out in order to keep him mom's venture afloat. In a coming-of age story filled with identity exploration, first love, and a boy's desire to see his mother's dreams come true, Peter helps his mother with her imaginative schemes. In the last section, we find out that there is no happy ending for Ella; her ventures never succeeded quite as well as Peter led us to believe. Even though the last lines end with Ella's death, we feel she lives on in the fantastic, if not quite true, tales of Peter.

THE BOOK OF SPLENDOR
Frances Sherwood
-
2002

It is written, "For ye shall go out with joy." That was what she wished.

Frances Sherwood's *The Book of Splendor* is a historical novel set in 17th-century Prague. Though it's centered around the classic Jewish figure of Rabbi Loew and his mythical golem, the true main character of Sherwood's story is Rochel Werner. An 18-year-old seamstress, Rochel falls in love with the rabbi's golem Yossel. Rabbi Loew and Yossel are called upon by the evil Emperor Rudolph II, who believes that the rabbi may be able to make him immortal. By telling the emperor each of the Jews in his kingdom holds a unique part of the immortality spell, the Rabbi protects his people from slaughter. While for the Jewish people it is an end that points toward peace, for Rochel, it is an ending that breaks her heart. Yossel perishes in the novel's climax, and Rochel must go on living. In the last lines, comfortable in her old age and reflecting on the times she spent in the synagogue, Rochel is staring at a candlestick holder that prophesied her future. Despite the pain surrounding her life, she hopes that she too can find peace like Yossel.

THE FORTRESS OF SOLITUDE
Jonathan Lethem
-
2003

Side by side, not truly quiet but quiescent, two gnarls of human scribble, human cipher, human dream.

Beginning in 1970s Brooklyn, Jonathan Lethem's *The Fortress of Solitude* spans nearly three decades of history and pop cultural development as we follow the protagonist, Dylan Ebdus, from childhood to adulthood. The thematic issue of racial tension is explored in the form of the childhood friendship between Dylan and a black boy named Mingus. United through a shared interest in superheroes, their relationship devolves as both boys grow older; Dylan moves out of Brooklyn and Mingus is left behind to struggle through the gentrification of his neighborhood. It is a transition that is difficult to swallow, leaving both men shells of their former selves as they move from childhood naivety to the harsh reality of adulthood. In the end, Dylan reflects on a seemingly insignificant moment of his youth as he rode in a car with his father, both nothing more than a tangled collection of ideas about what it means to be human.

LOVE AND OTHER GAMES OF CHANCE

Lee Siegel

-

2003

"Well" the editor finally sighed, "I suppose we could release it as a novel."

Lee Siegel's ambitious "novel" *Love and Other Games of Chance* is really more of a board game. At least, that is what his mother says. Presented as a mysterious box left by Lee Siegel's "real" father, Isaac Schlossberg, the novel's structure follows the layout of the game "Snakes & Ladders." Each of the 100 stories represents a square on the board, and the reader is free to travel through the narrative in any order they wish. The end result is a wildly embellished story of a man who is larger than life. Schlossberg was the first man on top of Mount Everest, traveled the world with the circus, and seduced dozens of women around the globe, if we are to believe him, of course. Embellishments abound, and, like the editor who utters the defeated final lines of the book, we too are left wondering what exactly we have just read.

THE TIME TRAVELER'S WIFE
Audrey Niffenegger
-
2003

He is coming, and I am here.

Audrey Niffenegger's debut novel, *The Time Traveler's Wife*, tells the story of a man who struggles to stay with the woman he loves because of a genetic disease that causes him to travel through time without warning. Regardless of his immensely inconvenient condition, Henry DeTamble manages to find love in a woman named Clare Abshire. In a novel that takes the idea of chronological events very loosely, Henry finds himself appearing in different places along Clare's time line, allowing him to become part of her life even while absent from her present. Provided with a list of future dates, Clare can track when Henry will appear, though these dates themselves are as loosely followed as time itself in the novel. When Henry dies, Clare's broken heart never mends. She waits the rest of her life in the hope that Henry will return. In the last lines, the reader is left with the sense that Henry is not going to return in the current timeline, but Clare will continue to wait no matter what.

THE KITE RUNNER
Khaled Hosseini
-
2003

I ran with the wind blowing in my face, and a smile as wide as the valley of Panjsher on my lips. I ran.

In Khaled Hosseini's debut novel, *The Kite Runner*, Afghanistan is depicted both prior to and during Taliban rule. The novel provides readers of all cultures with a realistic look into the lesser known aspects of the country's history. The protagonist, Amir, spends his childhood flying kites with his friend Hassan. After Hassan is brutalized by a bully while Amir stands by and does nothing, Amir and Hassan part ways. Forced to flee Afghanistan, Amir restarts his life in Pakistan. After learning Hassan has passed away, Amir rescues Hassan's son, Sohrab, and adopts him as his own. In the last scene, Amir and Sohrab fly a kite together, signifying Amir's absolution of his past failures and strengthening his connection with Sohrab. Free of their past, they are both as light as a kite on the wind.

SUITE FRANÇAISE
Irène Némirovsky
-
2004

The men began singing, a grave slow song that drifted away into the night. Soon the road was empty. All that remained of the German regiment was a little cloud of dust.

Irène Némirovsky intended *Suite Française* to be a series of five novels, however, she was only able to finish two before she was arrested during the Nazi occupation in France for being Jewish. Eventually, she was sent to Auschwitz and killed on August 17, 1942. In that sense, the series does not have a true ending and all we have is what Némirovsky wrote. Her work of historical fiction tells the story of Parisian characters as they try to escape France following the German invasion in 1940. The second novel in the collection, *Dolce*, ends with the victorious German soldiers rolling out of Paris, laden with supplies, leaving behind only a lingering cloud of dust. The ending offers no escape for the characters, an uncanny reflection of the author's own fate.

LET THE RIGHT ONE IN
John Ajvide Lindqvist
-
2004

If Stefan had been sitting there with that much luggage he would hardly have looked so happy. *But then, it's probably different when you're young.*

John Lindqvist's *Let the Right One In* takes place in a dreary Stockholm. It is a place that sucks the life out of people long before Eli, the vampire protagonist, can even get to them; still, that does not stop him from contributing. Eli, who is trapped as a 12-year-old for all of eternity, lives with a man who acts as his caretaker, fetching blood to keep Eli alive. Oskar, Eli's 12-year-old neighbor, becomes fascinated with Eli. They form a bond, and eventually Oskar is let in on the vampire's secret. The caretaker attempts to assault Eli and is killed, and Oskar runs away on a train with Eli tucked safely away in his luggage. It seems like a happy ending, but the reader is left with the sinking suspicion that Eli is merely grooming a new caretaker.

THE DARK TOWER VII: THE DARK TOWER

Stephen King

-

2004

> *"The man in black fled across the desert, and the gunslinger followed."*

Stephen King's *The Dark Tower VII*, the finale of the Dark Tower series, ends without a real resolution. Roland Deschain, the gunslinger and protagonist of the series, reaches the top of the Dark Tower, the place which holds all universes together, after an intense battle. Roland finds a door bearing his name and is pushed through by the tower itself. In a frustrating turn of events, Roland is thrown back to the very beginning of his journey, a fate the reader learns has happened to him hundreds of times. But Roland is not doomed to repeat his past failures. This time, equipped with the Horn of Eld, he may finally be able to break free of the loop he has been trapped in. The novel ends on the first line of the series. It is both a comforting and frustrating conclusion; one that provides few answers but leaves the reader with a glimmer of hope in an otherwise dreary turn of events.

10:01
Lance Olsen
-
2005

Milo Magnani glows with quiet pride, gives their thoughts back to these people, and, straightening his bowtie unnecessarily, rises to depart. Around him, throats clear, feet scrape, candy wrappers crinkle. The world grows brighter and brighter and brighter. Milo inhales and exhales. He waits. The film begins.

The vignettes within Lance Olsen's experimental novel *10:01* follow a cast of around 50 characters. The only connecting thread of plot is that every character is sitting in auditorium number 10 at the AMC theater in the Mall of America watching the 10 minutes of trailers that precede an unnamed movie. As a result, the novel is only made up of the scattered thoughts of the moviegoers. With characters ranging from an aerobics instructor to a serial killer, Olsen's snippets of American life come and go as quickly as the movie trailers. We are left with the closing thoughts of Milo Magnani, an assistant manager of the mall, who soaks up the ephemeral thoughts of his customers. Much like Milo, the reader is left to observe the people as they go about their lives—a cynical glimpse into the mindlessness of modern entertainment.

FRANK
R. M. Berry
-
2005

*Then its pages dampened, took on the weight of the underlying depths, began to founder, and as I readied to return home, that plot which had diverted so many, was finally **lost in darkness and distance.***

The final five words of R. M. Berry's *Frank* are exactly the same as the final five words of Mary Shelley's *Frankenstein*. Described as an "unwriting" of Mary Shelley's original horror classic, *Frank* tells the story of the student Frank Stein, who, while studying English at Harvard, writes an experimental work of fiction that he realizes could ruin his career. He chases the manuscript high and low, eventually ending up in the Florida Everglades. In the end, Stein does catch up to his printed words, but not before it's too late; what is written can never truly be erased.

GOD JR.
Dennis Cooper
-
2005

Let's say the extremely smooth grass in cemeteries is fake grass, and there is no one and nothing underneath it.

Dennis Cooper's *God Jr.* examines the psychological and emotional impact that the death of a child has on a parent. Jim and his teenage son, Tommy, were in a car accident that resulted in Tommy's death and left Jim wheelchair bound. Jim becomes locked in a state of arrested development; he blames himself for Tommy's death and tries desperately to regain a connection to his son through video games and marijuana. The stages of grief do not play out the same for everyone, and in Jim's case, they do not play out at all. He simply cannot come to terms with what has happened, so he finds a different way to carry on living: he pretends everything is all right.

THE RIGHT MADNESS
James Crumley
-
2005

The women tell me that after all these years I haven't even found myself. Of course, I haven't looked all that hard, yet.

C. W. Sughrue, James Crumley's hard-drinking and hard-hitting protagonist, returns in *The Right Madness*, the fourth and last novel to feature the character. Sughrue is an ex–army officer who works as a private investigator. When a new job comes up, he is hesitant to accept; the client, Dr. Will "Mac" Mackindrick, is not one to dole out simple tasks, after all. The case involves a number of confidential files stolen from the doctor's office, each as useful for blackmail as the next. In his quest to find the culprit, Sughrue pounds drinks and kills anyone who gets in his way, discovering that one of the doctor's patients was behind it all along. Justice is served and Sughrue returns home to continue on with his drug-taking, drink-swilling, cat-loving ways. The reader is left with the loose hope that, maybe, Sughrue will turn over a new leaf this time.

THE BOOK THIEF
Markus Zusak
-
2005

> *"A last note from your narrator: I am haunted by humans."*

The narrator who delivers the iconic last line in Markus Zusak's *The Book Thief* is none other than Death himself. In selecting the personified Death as his book's narrator, Zusak underlines the reality of human suffering in Germany during World War II. Zusak embodies Death with a surprising lack of menace, portraying a tired immortal who shepherds humanity through its own destruction. The novel follows Liesel Meminger, a young girl surrounded by the chaos of World War II. During the political and social unrest under Nazi rule, Liesel befriends Max, a Jewish refugee hidden in Liesel's foster parents' basement. Through the power of the written word, Liesel finds a glimmer of hope despite the encroaching destruction. At the end of the novel, Death, looking back on the depravity of humanity, leaves our world with a shiver of fear. A fitting reaction to the horrors brought about by war.

HOUSE OF MEETINGS
Martin Amis
-
2006

Join me, please, as I look on the bright side. Russia is dying. And I'm glad.

Martin Amis's *House of Meetings* tells the story of two brothers. The older, unnamed and with a history of brutality as a soldier, is the narrator of the story, recounting his life in a series of letters to his stepdaughter. The younger brother, Lev, is a poet and a diplomat. Both of them suffer in a Gulag prison camp during the last 10 years of Stalin's reign and both of them love Zoya, Lev's wife. The older brother tells his story in 2004, many years after he is released from the camp. The weariness felt by the old man as he details the horrible conditions of Soviet Russia is palpable, and even as he describes the love that both he and his brother feel for Zoya, it is nothing more than a weak tether, barely strong enough to anchor the men amidst the madness. At the end of his story, though, our gruff narrator can find a sliver of happiness: the Soviet Union fell, and with it, so did its suffering.

THE OPEN CURTAIN

Brian Evenson

-

2006

He waited for someone to tell him who to be next.

Possibly Brian Evenson's best known work, *The Open Curtain* deals with the transformation of the individual. The protagonist, Rudd Theurer, is a young Mormon who discovers his half brother, Lael, and becomes involved in a series of demented activities that ultimately culminate in murder. Fascinated with gore from a young age, Rudd finds himself obsessed with the idea of "blood atonement," a harrowing twist on the Christian redemption mythology that involves the cleansing of a guilty soul with another's blood. In a harrowing account of religious fervor, Evenson explores the idea of a forced identity and the effect of religious extremism on young children. In the final lines, Rudd is left incomprehensible and in shock, waiting for someone to tell him what he should become.

HARRY POTTER AND THE DEATHLY HALLOWS
J. K. Rowling
-
2007

The scar had not pained Harry for nineteen years.
All was well.

After seven long books, years of battle against Lord Voldemort, and a death and resurrection, Harry Potter finally wins. Initially, the final line was to be "Only those who he loved could see the lightning scar," but J. K. Rowling felt that this did not provide the finality she was after. Throughout Harry's entire life, the famous lightning bolt scar on his forehead pained him; it was a constant reminder that Voldemort was still on the move. As long as that scar caused him discomfort, the reader knew that Voldemort might rise again. By stripping it of that pain, Rowling made clear that the fighting was over; Voldemort was finally dead. After a childhood of chaos and pain, Harry is able to find peace at long last.

A THOUSAND SPLENDID SUNS
Khaled Hosseini
-
2007

But the naming game involves only male names, because if it's a girl, Laila has already named her.

In *A Thousand Splendid Suns*, Khaled Hosseini's much anticipated follow-up to *The Kite Runner*, Hosseini explores many of the same cultural topics as his first novel, but this time he does so from the female perspective. The story has been praised for its stark portrayal of the mistreatment of women in some Muslim countries. Laila, one of the two main characters of the novel, is at last able to reunite with her childhood love, Tariq, near the end of the novel. But true to the nature of the harsh world housing the narrative, their reunion is brief, as Tariq is forced to flee the war-torn country of Afghanistan. The close of the novel finds Laila, though injured, remaining steadfast and optimistic as she considers the child who resulted from her fleeting love affair with Tariq.

A VISIT FROM
THE GOON SQUAD
Jennifer Egan
-
2010

A sound of clicking heels on the pavement punctured the quiet. Alex snapped open his eyes, and he and Bennie both turned—whirled, really, peering for Sasha in the ashy dark. But it was another girl, young and new to the city, fiddling with her keys.

Jennifer Egan's *A Visit from the Goon Squad* redefined non-linear narrative. Tracking the lives of a number of individuals involved in the music industry, the story features a depth of character that many linear novels fail to achieve. By jumping through time, each character is given space to develop attachments to one another without the constraints imposed by a linear narrative. In the final chapter, we see the novel's more prominent characters as they find their place in the world. Desperate for reconnection, Alex and Bennie decide to visit Sasha, Alex's date from the first chapter in the novel. But these expectations are shattered as the two men realize Sasha is far away from them, living another life in another time.

HOW TO GET FILTHY RICH IN RISING ASIA

Mohsin Hamid

-

2013

. . . You are ready, ready to die well, ready to die like a man, like a woman, like a human, for despite all else you have loved, you have loved your father and your mother and your brother and your sister and your son and yes, your ex-wife, and you have loved the pretty girl, you have been beyond yourself, and so you have courage, and you have dignity, and you have calmness in the face of terror, and awe, and the pretty girl holds your hand, and you contain her, and this book, and me writing it, and I too contain you, who may not yet even be born, you inside me inside you, though not in a creepy way, and so may you, may I, may we, so may we all of us confront the end.

Mohsin Hamid's novel *How to Get Filthy Rich in Rising Asia* uses the second person to place "you," the reader, within the narrative. Your life begins in the slums of an unnamed country, and your journey takes you through the pursuit of education, happiness, love, immense success, and eventually, death. The final sentences add a universality to your experience, and like the characters you met along the way, you recognize that you are part of a unified human experience. As you pass on, you reach a sense of oneness with the universe, surrounded by the love and experience of every human being. It is an ambitious ending, and one that sticks with the reader long after the book has closed.

ment. I am thinking of aurochs and angels, the secret of dural
gments, prophetic sonnets, the refuge of art. And this is t
ly immortality you and I may share, my Lolita. | But I reck
got to light out for the Territory ahead of the rest, becau
it Sally she's going to adopt me and sivilize me and I car
and it. I been there before. | As you from crimes would pardor
, Let

WORKS CITED

artled by the overhead light, flew a large nocturnal butterf
at began circling the room. The strains of the piano and viol
se up weakly from below. | He loved Big Brother. | Ah Bartleb
humanity! ... or me to fe
ss alone, I had only to wish that there be a large crowd
ectators the day of my execution and that they greet me wi
ies of hate. | Are there any questions? | A sound of clicki
els o ... en h
es, and he and Bennie both turned-whirled, really, peering i
sha in the ashy dark. But it was another girl, young and r
the city, fiddling with her keys. | Don't ever tell anybo
ything. If you do, you start missing everybody. | After a whi
vent out and left the hospital and walked back to the hotel
e rain. | But wherever they go, and whatever happens to th
the way, in that enchanted place on the top of the Forest,
ttle boy and his Bear will always be playing. | He heard t
ng of steel against steel as a far door clanged shut. | Te
how free I am | He never sleeps, the judge. He is dancin
ncing. He says that he will never die. | But, in spite of the
ficiencies, the wishes, the hopes, the confdence, the predictic
the small band of true friends who witnessed the ceremony, we
lly answered in the perfect happiness of the union. | He w
on borne away by the waves and lost in darkness and distanc
The knife came down, missing him by inches, and he took off.
was the devious-cruising Rachel, that in her retracing sear
ter her missing children, only found another orphan. | In yo
cking-chair, by your window dreaming, shall you long, alone.
lingered round them, under that benign sky; watched the mot
tering among the heath, and hare-bells; listened to the soft wi

Works Cited

Candide
Voltaire. "Brutus." 1730.

The Life and Opinions of Tristram Shandy, Gentleman
Keymer, Thomas. *Laurence Sterne's Tristram Shandy: A Casebook.* Oxford University Press, 2006.

Timbs, John. "The Mirror of Literature, Amusement, and Instruction." *Mirror Monthly,* 1840.

Emma
Eggleston, Robert. "Emma, the Movies, and First-Year Literature Classes." *Persuasions.* Fall 1999.

Frankenstein
Poole, Buzz. "The Many Looks of Death." Printmag.com. 03 Jan. 2018. Web. Accessed 02 July 2018.

Père Goriot
Schermund, Elizabeth. "Rastignac." Blogs.transparent.com/french. 25 July 2016. Web. Accessed 02 July 2018.

Wuthering Heights
"Contemporary Reviews of *Wuthering Heights.*" Wuthering -heights.co.uk/reviews. Web. Accessed 02 July 2018.

Vanity Fair
Faulks, Sebastian. *Faulks on Fiction: Great British Heroes and the Secret Life of the Novel.* BBC Books, 2011.

Moby-Dick
"Herman Melville." *Encyclopaedia Britannica.* 03 Aug. 2017. Web. Accessed 02 July 2018.

McNearney, Allison. "Whatever Happened to the Book Herman Melville Wrote After 'Moby-Dick,'" Thedailybeast.com. 28 Apr. 2018. Web. Accessed 02 July 2018.

Bartleby, the Scrivener
Cornwell, Ethel. "Bartleby the Absurd." *The International Fiction Review,* 1982.

Barchester Towers
Sutherland, John. "An Introduction to Barchester Towers." Bl.uk. 15 May 2014. Web. Accessed 02 July 2018.

Les Misérables
Langeness, David. "*Les Misérables* at a Century and a Half." Pastemagazine .com. 18 Dec. 2012. Web. Accessed 02 July 2018.

Alice's Adventures in Wonderland
Rooney, Kathleen. "'Alice's Adventures in Wonderland' still inspires readers 150 years on." *The Chicago Tribune.* 19 Nov. 2015. Web. Accessed 02 July 2018.

Middlemarch
McCrum, Robert. "The 100 best novels: No. 21 – Middlemarch by George Eliot." *The Guardian.* 10 Feb. 2014. Web. Accessed 02 July 2018.

Middlemarch *cont.*

Armknecht, Megan. "The Weight of 'Glory': Emily Dickinson, George Eliot, and Women's Issues in Middlemarch." *Criterion: A Journal of Literary Criticism, Vol. 9, Issue 1.* 2016.

The Brothers Karamazov

Vonnegut, Kurt. *Slaughterhouse-Five.* Delacorte Press, 1969.

The Adventures of Huckleberry Finn

Norwood, Irvin. "The Adventures of Huckleberry Finn." Freebooksummary.com. Web. Accessed 02 July 2018.

Dracula

McCrum, Robert. "The 100 best novels: No. 31 – Dracula by Bram Stoker." *The Guardian.* 10 Feb. 2014. Web. Accessed 02 July 2018.

Miller, Elizabeth. "Original (deleted) ending of Bram Stoker's Dracula." Dracula.cc/literature. 10 May 2007. Web. Accessed 02 July 2018.

McTeague

Alioto, Daisy. "Stephen King's 10 favorite books." *The Christian Science Monitor.* 20 Jan. 2012. Web. Accessed 02 July 2018.

Sister Carrie

McCrum, Robert. "The 100 best novels: No. 33 – Sister Carrie by Theodore Dreiser." *The Guardian.* 05 May 2014. Web. Accessed 02 July 2018.

The Wonderful Wizard of Oz

"Following the Yellow Brick Road Back to the Origins of 'Oz.'" *All Things Considered. NPR.* 04 Apr. 2015. Web. Accessed 02 July 2018.

"The Wizard of Oz: An American Fairy Tale." Library of Congress. Web. Accessed 02 July 2018.

The Wings of the Dove

Thurber, James. "The Wings of Henry James." *The New Yorker.* 07 Nov. 1959.

The Call of the Wild

"Jack London." Biography.com. 02 Apr. 2014. Web. Accessed 02 July 2018.

Ethan Frome

Trilling, Lionel. *A Gathering of Fugitives.* Harcourt, 1978.

Swann's Way

Heffer, Simon. "How Proust's 'madeleine moment' changed the world forever." *The Telegraph.* 27 Oct. 2015. Web. Accessed 02 July 2018.

Of Human Bondage

McCrum, Robert. "The 100 best novels: No. 44 – Of Human Bondage by W. Somerset Maugham." *The Guardian.* 05 May 2014. Web. Accessed 02 July 2018.

A Portrait of the Artist as a Young Man

Bowker, Gordon. *James Joyce: A New Biography.* Farrar, Straus & Giroux, 2013.

Women in Love
Jacobson, Howard. "Contest with nature." *The Guardian*. 13 June 2008. Web. Accessed 02 July 2018.

Cane
Byrd, Rudolph P. *The World Has Changed: Conversations with Alice Walker*. The New Press, 2010.

Ford, Karen Jackson. *Split-Gut Song: Jean Toomer and the Poetics of Modernity*. University of Alabama Press, 2005.

The Trial
"The Trial." *Encyclopaedia Britannica*. 06 March 2017. Web. Accessed 02 July 2018.

The Sun Also Rises
McConnell, Molli. "Following in the Steps of Paris' Lost Generation." Theculturetrip.com. 20 Oct. 2016. Web. Accessed 02 July 2018.

Elmer Gantry
"Elmer Gantry, a Flawed Preacher for the Ages." *All Things Considered*. NPR.org. 22 Feb. 2008. Web. Accessed 02 July 2018.

The House at Pooh Corner
Ruggeri, Amanda. "AA Milne and the curse of Pooh bear." BBC.com. 28 Jan. 2016. Web. Accessed 02 July 2018.

Dodsworth
Ausmus, Martin. "Sinclair Lewis, *Dodsworth*, and the Fallacy of Reputation." *Books Abroad*. Autumn 1960.

Vile Bodies
Darbyshire, Neil. "An unhappy retreat into a happy ending." *The Telegraph*. 25 Aug. 2003. Web. Accessed 02 July 2018.

Brave New World
Aldous Huxley interviewed by Mike Wallace. 18 May 1958. The University of Texas, Austin, Texas.

Huxley, Aldous. *Letters of Aldous Huxley*. Harper & Row, 1969.

The Thin Man
"Nick, Nora (And Asta) Return in 'Thin Man' Novellas." *Weekend Edition Saturday*. NPR.org. 03 Nov. 2012. Web.

Tobacco Road
Garner, Dwight. "Pulp Valentine." Slate.com. 24 May 2006. Web. Accessed 02 July 2018.

Journey to the End of the Night
Fischer, Tibor. "Céline's journey to the cutting edge of literature." *The Guardian*. 15 June 2013. Web. Accessed 02 July 2018.

Miss Lonelyhearts
Rich, Nathaniel. "American Dreams, 1933: Miss Lonelyhearts by Nathanael West." Thedailybeast .com. 29 Apr. 2013. Web. Accessed 02 July 2018.

Nightwood
Austen, Roger. *Playing the Game: The Homosexual Novel in America*. Bobbs-Merrill, 1977.

Young, Ian. *The Male Homosexual in Literature: A Bibliography*. Scarecrow Press, 1975.

Of Mice and Men
Shillinglaw, Susan. "John Steinbeck."
The Guardian. 01 Feb. 2002. Web.
Accessed 02 July 2018.

Finnegans Wake
"Finnegans Wake." *Encyclopaedia
Britannica.* 16 Mar. 2017. Web.
Accessed 02 July 2018.

Mills, Billy. "Finnegans Wake – the
book the web was invented for."
The Guardian. 28 Apr. 2015. Web.
Accessed 02 July 2018.

Southam, B.C. *James Joyce.*
Routledge, 2013.

The Day of the Locust
Bramley, Ellie-Violet. "The Day
of the Locust, by Nathanael West,
glamorously grotesque." *The
Guardian.* 30 Dec. 2013. Web.
Accessed 02 July 2018.

Native Son
Rayson, Ann. *Richard Wright's Life.*
Oxford University Press, 2000.

The Stranger
Berlins, Marcel. "What is it about
Albert Camus' The Outsider that
makes it such an enduring favourite
with men?" *The Guardian.* 11 Apr.
2006. Web. Accessed 02 July 2018.

Animal Farm
Orwell, George. "'Animal Farm':
What Orwell Really Meant." *The
New York Review of Books.* December
1946. Web. Accessed 03 July 2018.

All the King's Men
Barnes, Bart. "Author-Poet Robert
Penn Warren Dies." *Washington Post.*
16 Sept. 1989. Web. Accessed 03
July 2018.

Under the Volcano
McCrum, Robert. "The 100 best
novels: No. 68 – Under the Volcano."
The Guardian. 05 Jan. 2015. Web.
Accessed 03 July 2018.

Power, Chris. "Under the Volcano:
a modernist masterpiece." *The
Guardian.* 02 Nov. 2011. Web.
Accessed 03 July 2018.

The Plague
Vulliamy, Ed. "Albert Camus' The
Plague: a story for our, and all, times."
The Guardian. 05 Jan. 2015. Web.
Accessed 03 July 2018.

Cry, the Beloved Country
"Cry, the Beloved Country: Theme of
Race." Shmoop.com. 11 Nov. 2008.
Web. Accessed 03 July 2018.

The Makioka Sisters
Mizumura, Minae. "'The Makioka
Sisters': An Aberrant Masterpiece."
Huffingtonpost.com. 02 Apr. 2015.
Web. Accessed 03 July 2018.

Nineteen Eighty-Four
Jordison, Sam. "Do you really know
what 'Orwellian' means?" *The
Guardian.* 11 Nov. 2014. Web.
Accessed 03 July 2018.

The Catcher in the Rye
"The Private War of J.D. Salinger." *The
Weekend Edition Sunday.* NPR
.gov. 01 Sept. 2013. Web. Accessed 03
July 2018.

Invisible Man
Prescott, Orville. "Books of the Times." *New York Times*. 16 Apr. 1952. Web. Accessed 03 July 2018.

Charlotte's Web
White, E.B. "Death of a Pig." *The Atlantic*. January 1948. Web. Accessed 03 July 2018.

The Adventures of Augie March
"Finding Augie March." *The New Yorker*. 06 Oct. 2003. Web. Accessed 03 July 2018.

The Unnamable
Matovic, Tijana. "End-less deconstruction of the self in Samuel Beckett's novel The Unnamable." Academia.edu. 2015. Web. Accessed 03 July 2018.

The Long Goodbye
Coggins, Mark. "Writing the Long Goodbye." Markcoggins.com. Web. Accessed 03 July 2018.

Lord of the Flies
McCrum. "The 100 best novels: No. 74 – Lord of the Flies by William Golding." *The Guardian*. 16 Feb. 2015. Web. Accessed 03 July 2018.

Lolita
Hooton, Christopher. "In 1956, Vladimir Nabokov skewered everything wrong with the 'important' books and movies with a 'message' that plague today." *The Independent*. 05 Jan. 2017. Web. Accessed 03 July 2018.

The Recognitions
William Gaddis interviewed by Zoltán Abádi-Nagy. "The Art of Fiction No. 101." *Paris Review*. Winter 1987. Web. Accessed 03 July 2018.

The Tree of Man
Ashcroft, Bill. *Patrick White Centenary: The Legacy of a Prodigal Son*. Cambridge Scholars Publishing, 2014.

The Quiet American
"The Disquieting Resonance of 'The Quiet American'." *All Things Considered*. NPR.org. 21 Apr. 2008. Web. Accessed 03 July 2018.

Bang the Drum Slowly
Litsky, Frank. "Mark Harris, Author of 'Bang the Drum Slowly,' Is Dead at 84." *New York Times*. 02 June 2007. Web. Accessed 03 July 2018.

A Walk on the Wild Side
Flanagan, Richard. "Prophet of the neon wilderness." *The Telegraph*. 29 Jan. 2006. Web. Accessed 03 July 2018.

The Ginger Man
Campbell, James. "J.P. Donleavy obituary." *The Guardian*. 14 Sept. 2017. Web. Accessed 03 July 2018.

Murphy, Pauline. "Insertions Downstairs." Headstuff.org. 26 Apr. 2017. Web. Accessed 03 July 2018.

Ufberg, Ross. "A Visit to Donleavyland, Sixty Years After 'The Ginger Man'." *The New Yorker*. 11 June 2015. Web. Accessed 03 July 2018.

Rabbit, Run
John Updike interviewed by Charles Thomas Samuels. "The Art of Fiction No. 43." *Paris Review*. Winter 1968. Web. Accessed 03 July 2018.

To Kill a Mockingbird
"Harper Lee, 'To Kill a Mockingbird' author, dies at 89." *Tribune Media Wire*. 19 Feb. 2016. Web. Accessed 03 July 2018.

"The Enduring Legacy of Harper Lee and To Kill a Mockingbird." *Life*. 20 Feb. 2016.

The Moviegoer
Santella, Andrew. "My Childish, Unhealthy, Joyous Obsession With The Moviegoer." *The Atlantic*. 07 Mar. 2014. Web. Accessed 03 July 2018.

Catch-22
Dickson, Paul. "The top 10 words invented by writers." *The Guardian*. 19 Nov. 2014. Web. Accessed 03 July 2018.

Martin, Gary. "Catch-22." Phrases .org.uk. 2018. Web. Accessed 03 July 2018.

Rosenbaum, Ron. "Seeing Catch-22 Twice." Slate.com. 02 Aug. 2011. Web. Accessed 03 July 2018.

A Clockwork Orange
Melis, Matt. "The Real Cure: A Clockwork Orange's Missing Ending." Consequenceofsound.com. 09 Feb. 2015. Web. Accessed 03 July 2018.

Cat's Cradle
Arbeiter, M. "15 Things You Might Not Know About Cat's Cradle." Mentalfloss.com. 03 July 2015. Web.

Accessed 03 July 2018.

The Bell Jar
Moss, Howard. "Dying: An Introduction." *The New Yorker*. 10 July 1971. Web. Accessed 03 July 2018.

City of Night
Casillo, Charles. "Fifty Years of Rechy's 'City of Night'." *Los Angeles Review of Books*. 13 Oct. 2013. Web. Accessed 03 July 2018.

A Confederate General from Big Sur
Barber, John. "Comprehensive information about Richard Brautigan, his life, and writings." Brautigan. net. 23 June 2018. Web. Accessed 03 July 2018.

Second Skin
Beha, Christopher R. "Night Driving." *The Believer*. December 2004. Web. Accessed 03 July 2018.

A Moveable Feast
Yardley, Jonathan. "Ernest Hemingway's 'A Moveable Feast' Still Satisfies." *Washington Post*. 13 Dec. 2006. Web. Accessed 03 July 2018.

Giles Goat-Boy
Clavier, Berndt. *John Barth and Postmodernism: Spatiality, Travel, Montage*. Peter Lang Inc., 2006.

In Cold Blood
Pilkington, Ed. "In Cold Blood, half a century on." *The Guardian*. 15 Nov. 2009. Web. Accessed 03 July 2018.

Trout Fishing in America
"Brautigan's Surreal Story: 'Trout

Fishing in America.'" *Weekend Edition Saturday*. NPR.org. 06 Feb. 2010. Web. Accessed 03 July 2018.

One Hundred Years of Solitude
Jordison, Sam. "Reading group: One Hundred Years of Solitude is our book for May." *The Guardian*. 02 May 2017. Web. Accessed 03 July 2018.

Willie Masters' Lonesome Wife
"Willie Masters' Lonesome Wife." Dalkeyarchive.com. Web. Accessed 03 July 2018.

Them
Burns, Carole. "Off the Page: Joyce Carol Oates." *Washington Post*. 24 Oct. 2003. Web. Accessed 03 July 2018.

Slaughterhouse-Five
Lehmann-Haupt, Christopher. "Slaughterhouse-Five, Or the Children's Crusade." *New York Times*. 31 Mar. 1969. Web. Accessed 03 July 2018.

Another Roadside Attraction
Robbins, Tom. *Tibetan Peach Pie: A True Account of an Imaginative Life*. Ecco, 2014.

All My Friends Are Going to Be Strangers
Harrison, Jim. "All My Friends Are Going to Be Strangers." *New York Times*. 19 Mar. 1972. Web. Accessed 03 July 2018.

Crash
Smith, Zadie. "Sex and wheels: Zadie Smith on J.G. Ballard's Crash." *The Guardian*. 04 July 2014. Web.

Accessed 03 July 2018.

Gravity's Rainbow
Beausang, Chris. "Thomas Pynchon's 'Gravity's Rainbow' and the difficulty of endings." Medium.com. 16 Apr. 2017. Web. Accessed 03 July 2018.

Kihss, Peter. "Pulitzer Jurors Dismayed on Pynchon." *New York Times*. 08 May 1974. Web. Accessed 03 July 2018.

Mrs. October Was Here
Coleman Dowell interviewed by John O'Brien. Dalkeyarchive.com. 1982. Web. Accessed 03 July 2018.

The Hair of Harold Roux
Ulin, David. "Book review: 'The Hair of Harold Roux' by Thomas Williams." *Los Angeles Times*. 19 June 2011. Web. Accessed 03 July 2018.

The Ebony Tower
Lehmann-Haupt, Christopher. "More Magic from John Fowles." *New York Times*. 04 Nov. 1974. Web. Accessed 03 July 2018.

Song of Solomon
Toni Morrison interview by Christopher Bollen. *Interview*. 01 May 2012. Web. Accessed 03 July 2018.

Arthur Rex
Giardina, Henry. "Thomas Berger's Egoless Fictions." *The New Yorker*. 30 July 2014. Web. Accessed 03 July 2018.

The Book of Laughter and Forgetting
Updike, John. "The Most Original Book of the Season." *New York Times*. 30 Nov. 1980. Web. Accessed 03 July 2018.

Mulligan Stew
Gioia, Ted. "Mulligan Stew." Postmodernmystery.com. 23 Aug. 2011. Web. Accessed 03 July 2018.

How German Is It
Updike, John. "Sentimental Re-Education." *The New Yorker*. 16 Feb. 2004. Web. Accessed 03 July 2018.

Housekeeping
McCrum, Robert. "The 100 best novels: No. 92 – Housekeeping by Marilynne Robinson." *The Guardian*. 22 June 2015. Web. Accessed 03 July 2018.

Distant Relations
Weiss, Jason. *Writing At Risk: Interviews in Paris with Uncommon Writers*. University of Iowa Press, 1991.

Waiting for the Barbarians
Aytemiz, Pelin. "Victims of the Empire: An Analysis on Coetzee's Waiting for the Barbarians." Academia.edu. 2016. Web. Accessed 03 July 2018.

A Confederacy of Dunces
Jordison, Sam. "A Confederacy of Dunces: a Pulitzer winner's struggle to find a publisher." *The Guardian*. 13 June 2017. Web. Accessed 03 July 2018.

The Transit of Venus
de Krester, Michelle. "Book of a lifetime: The Transit of Venus by Shirley Hazzard." *The Independent*. 08 Mar. 2013. Web. Accessed 03 July 2018.

Robinson, Roxana. "Love Story Electrifies Beneath the Silhouette 'Of Venus'." NPR.org. 15 Sept. 2013. Web. Accessed 03 July 2018.

Midnight's Children
"An Epic of India Gets a Canvas Its Own Size." *Morning Edition*. NPR.org. 09 May 2013. Web. Accessed 03 July 2018.

Oh What a Paradise It Seems
Leonard, John. "Cheever Country." *New York Times*. 07 Mar. 1982. Web. Accessed 03 July 2018.

The Color Purple
Edemariam, Aida. "Free spirit." *The Guardian*. 23 June 2007. Web. Accessed 03 July 2018.

The Names
Foster, Graham. "The Names by Don DeLillo." Grahamfoster.com. 03 May 2016. Accessed 04 July 2018.

Angels
Gourevitch, Philip. "'What a Pair of Lungs!' Denis Johnson's Ecstatic American Voice." *The New Yorker*. 27 May 2017. Web. Accessed 04 July 2018.

Hoffman, Alice. "Slumps and Tailspins." *New York Times*. 02 Oct. 1983. Web. Accessed 04 July 2018.

The Name of the Rose
Eco, Umberto. *The Name of the Rose.*
Harcourt, 1984.

The Unbearable Lightness of Being
Banville, John. "Light but sound:
John Banville rereads The Unbearable
Lightness of Being." *The Guardian.*
30 Apr. 2004. Web. Accessed 04
July 2018.

Hansen, John. "'The Ambiguity and
Existentialism of Human Sexuality
in *The Unbearable Lightness of Being.*'"
Philosophicalpathways.com. 11 June
2015. Web. Accessed 04 July 2018.

White Noise
McCrum, Robert. "Don DeLillo:
'I'm not trying to manipulate
reality – this is what I see and hear.'"
The Guardian. 07 Aug. 2010. Web.
Accessed 04 July 2018.

Perfume: The Story of a Murderer
Markham, James. "Success of Smell
Is Sweet for New German Novelist."
New York Times. 09 Oct. 1986. Web.
Accessed 04 July 2018.

Continental Drift
Lee, Don. "About Russell Banks: A
Profile." *Ploughshares.* Winter 1993.
Web. Accessed 04 July 2018.

Schuessler, Jennifer. "The Artist and
the Upper Class." *The New York
Review of Books.* 20 Mar. 2008. Web.
Accessed 04 July 2018.

Always Coming Home
Ursula LeGuin interviewed by
Michael Brayndick. Ir.uiowa.edu.
1986. Web. Accessed 04 July 2018.

Rat Man of Paris
Segal, Lore. "The Flasher of the
Apocalypse." *New York Times.* 16
Feb. 1986.

Paul West interviewed by David W.
Madden. Dalkeyarchive.com. 1991.
Web. Accessed 04 July 2018.

The Handmaid's Tale
Atwood, Margaret. "Haunted by The
Handmaid's Tale." *The Guardian.*
20 Jan. 2012. Web. Accessed 04
July 2018.

Christopher Unborn
Ruta, Suzanne. "Nine Months That
Shook the World." *New York Times.*
20 Aug. 1989. Web. Accessed 04
July 2018.

The Broom of the System
Max, D.T. "The Unfinished." *The
New Yorker.* 09 Mar. 2009. Web.
Accessed 04 July 2018.

The Messiah of Stockholm
Grossman, David. "The Age of
Genius." *The New Yorker.* 08 June
2009. Web. Accessed 04 July 2018.

You Bright and Risen Angels
William T. Vollmann interviewed by
Larry McCaffery. Dalkeyarchive.com.
1993. Web. Accessed 04 July 2018.

The Carpathians
King, Michael. "Janet Frame." *The
Guardian.* 30 Jan. 2004. Web.
Accessed 04 July 2018.

Stoner
"Stoner by John Williams awarded
Waterstones book prize." BBC.com.
03 Dec. 2013. Web. Accessed 04
July 2018.

Stoner *cont.*
Hampson, Sarah. "Stoner: How the story of a failure became an all-out publishing success." *Globe and Mail.* 07 Dec. 2013. Web. Accessed 04 July 2018.

Prisoner's Dilemma
Eder, Richard. "What Is Dad Trying to Tell Us?" *Los Angeles Times.* 20 Mar. 1988. Web. Accessed 04 July 2018.

Hegi, Ursula. "What's the Matter with Eddie?" *New York Times.* 13 Mar. 1988. Web. Accessed 04 July 2018.

Cat's Eye
Fragoso, Margaux. "Teen Girls, Mean Girls: A Tale of Karmic Revenge." NPR.org. 30 Jan. 2012. Web. Accessed 04 July 2018.

Arrogance
Chu, Christie. "8 Things That Will Change the Way You Think About Egon Schiele." Artnet.com. 12 June 2015. Web. Accessed 04 July 2018.

Jones, Jonathan. "The come-on." *The Guardian.* 19 Apr. 2003. Web. Accessed 04 July 2018.

Things in the Night
Esposito, Scott. "Things in the Night." Raintaxi.com. 2006. Web. Accessed 04 July 2018.

The Art Lover
Carole Maso interviewed by Stephen Moore. Dalkeyarchive.com. 1997. Web. Accessed 04 July 2018.

Harlot's Ghost
"Harlot's Ghost." *Publishers Weekly.* 30 Sept. 1991. Web. Accessed 04 July 2018.

Orion in The Return of Painting, The Pearl, and Orion: A Trilogy
Leslie Scalapino interviewed by Maggie Golston at the University of Arizona Poetry Center. Poetry. arizona.edu. 03 Nov. 2015. Web. Accessed 04 July 2018.

A Thousand Acres
Steiner, Susie. "Book of a lifetime: A Thousand Acres, by Jane Smiley." *The Independent.* 12 Apr. 2013. Web. Accessed 04 July 2018.

The Runaway Soul
Jaffe, Harold. "An I for an I." *Los Angeles Times.* 10 Nov. 1991. Web. Accessed 05 July 2018.

The Shipping News
Jordison, Sam. "The Shipping News: Concluding questions." *The Guardian.* 19 Dec. 2011. Web. Accessed 05 July 2018.

In a Country of Mothers
Cochrane, Kira. "A.M. Homes interview: 'I write the things we don't want to say out loud.'" *The Guardian.* 07 June 2013. Web. Accessed 05 July 2018.

The Eye in the Door
"The Eye in the Door." *Publishers Weekly.* 02 May 1994. Web. Accessed 05 July 2018.

Sabbath's Theatre
Specktor, Matthew. "A Gruesome 'Sabbath': Roth's Vile, Brilliant Masterpiece." NPR.org. 03 Dec. 2012. Web. Accessed 05 July 2018.

The Green Mile
Hendrix, Grady. "The Great Stephen King Reread: The Green Mile." Tor .com. 19 June 2015. Web. Accessed 05 July 2018.

Infinite Jest
Holub, Christian. "'Infinite Jest' celebrates 20th anniversary." 26 Feb. 2016. Web. Accessed 05 July 2018.

Dra—
"Stacey Levine with Kristy Eldredge." *The Brooklyn Rail.* 01 June 2017. Web. Accessed 05 July 2018.

Memoirs of a Geisha
Arthur Golden interviewed by Miles O'Brien. "A talk with Arthur Golden." CNN. 23 Mar. 1999. Web. Accessed 05 July 2018.

Panther in the Basement
"Panther in the Basement." *Kirkus Reviews.* 01 Aug. 1997. Web. Accessed 05 July 2018.

Charming Billy
Olsen, Diane. *The Book That Changed My Life.* Modern Library, 2002. Accessed 05 July 2018.

The Wind-Up Bird Chronicle
Bausells, Marta. "Haruki Murakami: 'My lifetime dream is to be sitting at the bottom of a well.'" *The Guardian.* 24 Aug. 2014. Web. Accessed 05 July 2018.

Motherless Brooklyn
Jonathan Lethem interviewed by Jay MacDonald. Bookpage.com. September 2003. Web. Accessed 05 July 2018.

Brokeback Mountain
"An Interview with Annie Proulx." *The Missouri Review.* 1999. Web. Accessed 05 July 2018.

Portrait of an Artist, as an Old Man
Adams, Tim. "What's the catch?" *The Guardian.* 29 July 2000. Web. Accessed 05 July 2018.

Blonde
Lambert, Brent. "Joyce Carol Oates and David Fincher Join Forces with Brad Pitt for a Brilliant Plan B Dream Team." Feelguide.com. 03 Oct. 2013. Web. Accessed 05 July 2018.

By Night in Chile
Gutiérrez-Mouat, Ricardo. *Understanding Roberto Bolaño.* University of South Carolina Press, 2016. Accessed 05 July 2018.

The Final Country
"James Crumley." *Encyclopaedia Britannica.* 02 Nov. 2015. Web. Accessed 05 July 2018.

White Teeth
Chotiner, Isaac. "Zadie Smith on Male Critics, Appropriation, and What Interests Her Novelistically About Trump." Slate.com. 16 Nov. 2016. Web. Accessed 05 July 2018.

Moss, Stephen. "White Teeth by Zadie Smith." *The Guardian.* 26 Jan.

2000. Web. Accessed 05 July 2018.

Requiem
Seaman, Donna. "Curtis White tests the limits with 'Requiem.'" *Chicago Tribune.* 13 Jan. 2002. Web. Accessed 05 July 2018.

Fixer Chao
Benfer, Amy. "'Fixer Chao' by Han Ong." Salon.com. 19 Apr. 2001. Web. Accessed 05 July 2018.

Life of Pi
Stewart, Jeannette. "Obama sends Yann Martel Life of Pi appreciation letter." *National Post.* 06 Apr. 2010. Web. Accessed 05 July 2018.

Middlesex
O'Hehir, Andrew. "'Middlesex' by Jeffrey Eugenides." Salon.com. 05 Sept. 2002. Web. Accessed 05 July 2018.

Ciabattari, Jane. "The 21st Century's 12 greatest novels." BBC.com 19 Jan. 2015. Web. Accessed 05 July 2018.

The Lovely Bones
Smith, Ali. "A perfect afterlife." *The Guardian.* 16 Aug. 2002. Web. Accessed 05 July 2018.

Inflating a Dog: The Story of Ella's Lunch Launch
Gaskell, Betsy. "An Interview with the Author." Erickraft.com. 2007. Web. Accessed 05 July 2018.

The Time Traveler's Wife
Zambreno, Kate. "Audrey Niffenegger: Woman on the edge of time." *The Independent.* 23 Jan. 2004. Web. Accessed 05 July 2018.

The Kite Runner
Milvy, Erika. "The 'Kite Runner' controversy." Salon.com. 09 Dec. 2007. Web. Accessed 05 July 2018.

Suite Française
Gray, Paul. "As France Burned." *New York Times.* 09 Apr. 2006. Web. Accessed 05 July 2018.

Shakespeare, Nicholas. "The Life of Irène Némirovsky, 1903-1942 by Olivier Philipponnat and Patrick Lienhardt: review." *The Telegraph.* 12 Feb. 2010. Web. Accessed 05 July 2018.

10:01
Martin, Stephen-Paul. "Already Too Many Stories in the World." Electronicbookreview.com. 22 Sept. 2006. Web. Accessed 05 July 2018.

Frank
"R. M. Berry. Frank." *Review of Contemporary Fiction.* 2006. Thefreelibrary.com. Web. Accessed 05 July 2018.

The Book Thief
Markus Zusak interviewed by Heidi Stillman at the Chicago Public Library. Chipublib.org. Spring 2012. Web. Accessed 05 July 2018.

A Visit from the Goon Squad
Gallagher, Paul. "Interview: Jennifer Egan on A Visit from the Goon Squad." Scottishbooktrust.com. Web. Accessed 05 July 2018.

Fulford, Robert. "Jennifer Egan's A Visit from the Goon Squad is all about the timing." *National Post.* 10 Jan. 2012. Web. Accessed 05 July 2018.

rable pigments, prophetic sonnets, the refuge of art. And t]
reckon I got to light out for the Territory ahead of the res
can't stand it. I been there before. | As you from crimes wo
npshade, startled by the overhead light, flew a large nocturn
d violin rose up weakly from below. | He loved Big Brother. |
to feel less alone, I had only to wish that there be a larg
with cries of hate. | Are there any questions? | I shall 1
ll fruit of his writings, as I desired, because my only desir
chivalry, which thanks to the exploits of my real Don Quixc
the ground. Farewell.' | Don't ever tell anybody anything.
d left the hospital and walked back to the hotel in the rain
that enchanted place on the top of the Forest, a little boy
ainst steel as a far door clanged shut. | Tell me how free I
at he will never die. | But, in spite of these deficiencies,
nd of true friends who witnessed the ceremony, were fully an
ay by the waves and lost in darkness and distance. | The kni
/ious-cruising Rachel, that in her retracing search after her
your window dreaming, shall you long, alone. | I lingered r
e heath, and hare-bells; listened to the soft wind breathing th
imbers for the sleepers in that quiet earth. A last note from
ave slow song that drifted away into the night. Soon the roa
oud of dust. | The horizon is the straight bottom edge of a
/ farewell, farewell to Alexandria leaving. | That was all I
at hour that frogs begin and the scent off the mesquite come
ought, except maybe a little time between, nine months, and
stled among the broad sheets of paper. First one sheet, then
'From the land of Oz," said Dorothy gravely. "And here is Tot
st received the cross of the Legion of Honour. | "She's neve
e's as he is now!" | She sat staring with her eyes shut, intc
nething she couldn't begin, and she saw him moving farther an
e pin point of light. | This is the difference between this a
an listen I got this neat idea hey, you listening? Hey? You
ighed. He did not care what she called herself as long as sh
a would live. She would not leave him. | All these weirdos, a
iad never known, never even imagined for a heartbeat, that

is the only immortality you and I may share, my Lolita. | E

because Aunt Sally she's going to adopt me and sivilize me a

pardoned be, Let your indulgence set me free. | Up out of t

utterfly that began circling the room. The strains of the pia

Bartleby! Ah humanity! | For everything to be consummated, 1

rowd of ~~spectators~~ the ~~~~ ~~~~ and that they gre

proud ~~~~ ~~~~ to enjoy t

is been to make men hate those false, absurd histories in boc

are even now tottering, and without any doubt will soon tumb

ou do, you start mi~~~~ ~~~~ After a while I went c

But wherever they go ~~~~ ~~~~ to them on the wa

his Bear will always be playing. | He heard the ring of ste

| He never sleeps, the judge. He is dancing, dancing. He sa

wishes, the hopes, the confid~~~~ the ~~dictions~~ he sma

red in the ~~~~ ~~~~ on bor

INDEX

ame down, missing him by inches, and he took off. | It was t

sing children, only found another orphan. | In your rocking-cha

them, under that benign sky; watched the moths futtering amc

;h the grass; and wondered how any one could ever imagine unqu:

narrator: I am haunted by humans. | The men began singing,

s empty. All that remained of the German regiment was a litt

ain arbitrarily and suddenly lowered upon a performance. | A

ago in some brief lost spring, in a place that is no more.

trongest. | You been dead all your life since you was born,

you're dead. | On John Andrews's writing table the brisk wi

her, blew off the table, until the floor was littered with the

oo. And oh, Aunt Em! I'm so glad to be at home again! | He h

und peace since she left his arms, and never will again ti

s eyes, and felt as if she had finally got to the beginning

arther away, farther and farther into the darkness until he w

that. | We had the castle within us. We carried it away. | Sc

ening...? | Terminal. | No one remembers the whole story. |

nt on living. And she would do that. No matter where she wei

e getting a little better every day right in the midst of the

Index